Ritchie Blackmore
A Life In Vision

Ritchie Blackmore
A Life In Vision

Narrative by Jerry Bloom

WP
WYMER
PUBLISHING
Bedford, England

First published in Great Britain in 2019
by Wymer Publishing
www.wymerpublishing.co.uk
Tel: 01234 326691
Wymer Publishing is a trading name of Wymer (UK) Ltd

This edition copyright © 2023 Wymer Publishing.

ISBN: 978-1-915246-30-1

The Author hereby asserts his rights to be identified
as the author of this work in accordance with sections
77 to 78 of the Copyright, Designs & Patents Act 1988.

All rights reserved. No part of this publication may be
reproduced or transmitted in any form or by any means,
electronic or mechanical, including photocopying, or any
information storage and retrieval system, without written
permission from the publisher.

This publication is sold subject to the condition that it shall not,
by way of trade or otherwise, be lent, re-sold, hired out or
otherwise circulated without the publishers prior consent in any
form of binding or cover other than that in which it is published
and without a similar condition including this condition
being imposed on the subsequent purchaser.

Every effort has been made to trace the copyright holders of the
photographs in this book but some were unreachable. We would
be grateful if the photographers concerned would contact us.

Design by 1016 Sarpsborg
Printed by Halstan, Amersham, Buckinghamshire.

A catalogue record for this book is available from the British Library.

Contents

The Early Years: 1958-67	**9**
The Colour Purple: 1968-75	**45**
A New Spectrum: 1975-84	**65**
More Purple Passages: 1984-1993	**85**
Reflecting The Rainbow: 1994-1997	**103**
In The Shadow Of Times Past: 1997-	**109**

The Outlaws with Jerry Lee Lewis at Wallington Public Hall, 28th May 1963.

The Early Years: 1958-67

When researching for *Black Knight* one of the things I discovered was that in the very early days of Ritchie's career he had played in my hometown of Bedford. It inspired me to not only research other gigs in Bedford, but also set me on a path to try and document as many of Ritchie's gigs before he joined Deep Purple as possible.

Plenty of this information came to light during the research for *Black Knight* but much of it has also been compiled in the intervening years. Even though *Black Knight* included a discography, including his early years, a partial gig list from the same period seemed pointless. With other books and websites having documented Deep Purple and Rainbow gig lists it also seemed pointless to reproduce those again here, but at least now a fairly comprehensive list of his gigs before Purple are published for the first time.

Of course, it is not complete, and there are probably a few inaccuracies. Some of this data was collated with the huge help of many of the musicians who worked with Ritchie at the time. Sadly, since interviewing them in 2005, many of them have since passed on, making the job or researching additional information even more difficult.

Most of the gigs took place in England and where the county is listed, I have done so as they were at the time, before the boundary changes that occurred under the local Government Act of 1972. Some gigs may have been cancelled that I am not aware of and there are certainly others that I have yet to discover. Any gigs that there is uncertainty about, whether or not they went ahead, or whether or not Ritchie played on them, as well as gigs that were cancelled, are all listed in grey. But it is the most detailed list yet compiled with in excess of four hundred gigs that makes for fascinating reading.

The one major thing that occurred after the publication of *Black Knight* was being contacted by Bob Danks who corrected much of the information concerning the period before Ritchie's first professional gigs concerning the band names. He also supplied the magnificent Dominators' gig posters that are illustrated.

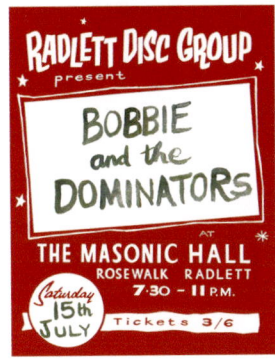 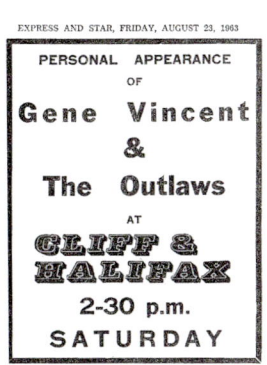 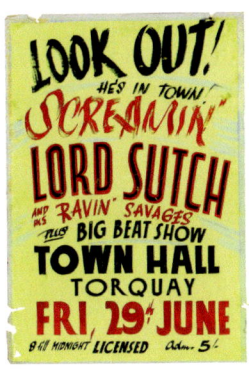  

1958 – The 21's Coffee Bar Junior Skiffle Group

Ritchie Blackmore - dog box, washboard
Glen Stoner - guitar
David Cox - guitar
David Rodham - guitar
Victor Hare - guitar

Whilst at Heston Senior School, Blackmore joined his first band. With numerous guitarists, Blackmore at 13 was not considered good enough to play guitar at this stage, having only been playing for two years. Instead he started on a dog box, before playing a washboard. There were thought to be other musicians including a couple of girl singers.

I have yet to document any gigs. They might have played at school, but beyond that it is unlikely that gigs elsewhere were done. There was apparently at least one other short-lived school group with fellow pal and guitarist, Barry Lovegrove.

(late Summer) 1958 – The Vampires

Bob Danks - rhythm guitar, lead vocals
Ritchie Blackmore - rhythm guitar
Dave Ronay - banjo
Mick Catherwood - tea-chest bass, vocals
Alan Dunklin - washboard

This is the band that Blackmore sometimes refers to (incorrectly) as The Satellites. The Satellites were in fact the band that Rodger Mingaye joined after leaving The Vampires. Danks, Mingaye, and Dunklin all went to Chiswick County Grammar school. Heston schoolboy Blackmore was drafted in through Dunklin, who lived next door but one to Blackmore in Ash Grove, Heston. The Vampires originally started as a Skiffle outfit but after Mingaye left they changed their musical style.

December 1958-June 1959 – The Electric Vampires

Bob Danks - rhythm guitar, lead vocals
Mick Cartwright - rhythm guitar, vocals
Ritchie Blackmore - lead guitar
Alan Dunklin - bass
Clive Buckie - drums

After Mingaye's departure they soon changed the name to reflect the change in musical direction. Blackmore also took over lead guitar duties.

1958

Date	Venue
Wednesday 24th December	Kings Head, Twickenham England

This was the band's debut gig on Christmas Eve 1958 although Bob Danks recalls that it was their first "paying" gig, so they may well have done a few prior to it. The band secured a residency in Twickenham, supplementing this with work at weddings and youth clubs, where they'd play rock 'n' roll standards such as Vince Taylor's 'Brand New Cadillac' and Shadows' numbers.

Left to right: Barry Lovegrove, Clive Buckie, Alan Dunklin and Ritchie.

June-December 1959 – The Dominators

Tony Parsons - lead vocals
Bob Danks - lead & rhythm guitar, vocals
Ritchie Blackmore - lead & rhythm guitar
Alan Dunklin - bass
Clive Buckie - drums
Mick Underwood - drums

Having evolved from The Vampires (they basically just changed the name!), Blackmore was insistent on having a non-guitar playing singer, so Tony Parsons was added to the line-up.

Bob Danks: "The Vampires became the 'Electric Vampires' then because Ritchie had a Watkins Dominator amp and I had a Norton Dominator motorcycle we changed the name!"

According to Danks' memory Buckie was replaced by Underwood for a while, before returning to the line-up. Bob Danks: "When we first started we had a policy of 'whoever learned an instrumental first' played it on stage. As I was at work and able to buy quite a few records to learn quickly, I often played lead with Ritchie on rhythm, then suddenly his ability to pick up solos just took off at a tremendous rate and I just could not compete. I carried on with rhythm and vocals."

1959

Date	Venue
Monday 3rd August	GEC Sports Pavilion, Wembley.

Billed as "The Dominators Swing Group".

1960-July 1961 – Bobbie & The Dominators

Bob Danks - lead vocals
Ritchie Blackmore - lead guitar
Barry Lovegrove - rhythm guitar
Alan Dunklin - bass
Clive Buckie - drums
Terry Maybey - drums

"Although I did most of the vocals we were always trying new singers. Tony Parsons was one of these. He then got a job which kept him away and not able to get to every gig so he left. This became frustrating as I was still doing most of the vocals so I dropped rhythm and we got Barry Lovegrove in as rhythm, although he was very good and occasionally played lead."

"The Dominators however used to feature 'Brand New Cadillac' in our set and it was always a compliment when people used to say that we did it better than Vince's Playboys. That was due to Ritchie already having started to become quite wild with his playing not because of my vocals!"

The drumming situation may have also continued with Underwood, depending on availability but also Terry Maybey occasionally stepped in.

The only dates documented so far are towards the end of his time with the band. Indeed, as you can see below, Blackmore joined the Jaywalkers in May but as the gig in Radlett shows, he was still doing gigs with the Dominators as well for a couple of months.

1961

Date	Venue
date unknown	Trinity Hall, Hounslow, Middlesex

Terry Maybey stepped in on drums.

Saturday 15th July	Masonic Hall, Radlett

Billed as Bobbie & The Dominators, one of the last gigs.

July	White Hart, Southall

May 1961-April 1962 – Mike Dee & The Jaywalkers

Mike Dee (Wheeler) - vocals
Ritchie Blackmore - guitar
Terry Mabey - drums (briefly replaced by Derek Sirmon)
David Tippler - bass
Brian Mansell - rhythm guitar

Mike Dee & The Jaywalkers were formed in February 1961 although the members had been active for some time before Mike Wheeler, who used the stage name Dee, joined as vocalist.

It was when Blackmore joined this band that he turned professional and gave up his day job at London Airport. He clearly was determined to make a career from music because the same month, having just turned 16 he had auditioned to join Screaming Lord Sutch & The Savages but lost out to Rodger Mingaye, whose place he had taken in The Vampires.

Come what may, like The Savages, The Jaywalkers had an extensive booking schedule. It was also shortly after joining The Jaywalkers that he got his Gibson ES-335.

Most of the dates here were unearthed by Sixties music archivist Nick Warburton and come from Brian Mansell's diary although it is stated that these are "selected" gigs so one can assume there were many more. Almost as soon as Mike Dee joined the band they auditioned at the Carlton in Slough, which secured them a weekly gig there.

Blackmore secured his place in the band thanks to the band's lead guitarist Brian Sell. Sell claims to have had met Blackmore at Dawe Instruments electronics factory in Brentford, Middlesex around 1959 where he said Blackmore worked, but if that is correct it was more likely to have been in 1960 as Blackmore was only 14 in 1959. The pair briefly rehearsed together in a trio with drummer Mick Underwood before Sell formed The Jaywalkers and Blackmore and (later) Underwood joined Bobbie & The Dominators.

Sell introduced Blackmore to The Jaywalkers but it cost Sell his place in the band because they were more impressed with Blackmore's playing.

The Jaywalkers got to perform at two shows on a Billy Fury tour as late replacements (see page 16) but they managed to get their photo taken with him backstage in Portsmouth. Left to right: Terry Mabey, Billy Fury, Brian Mansell, Mick Wheeler, Ritchie Blackmore and Dave Tippler, 21st November 1961.

1961

Date	Venue
Saturday 6th May	Essoldo, Slough, Berkshire
Wednesday 10th May	Carlton Ballroom, Slough, Berkshire
Saturday 13th May	White Hart, Southall, Middlesex
Wednesday 17th May	Carlton Ballroom, Slough, Berkshire
Sunday 21st May	Carlton Ballroom, Slough, Berkshire
Saturday 27th May	Essoldo, Slough, Berkshire
Wednesday 31st May	Carlton Ballroom, Slough, Berkshire

Saturday 3rd June	Staines Town Hall, Staines, Middlesex
Sunday 4th June	Carlton Ballroom, Slough, Berkshire
Wednesday 7th June	Carlton Ballroom, Slough, Berkshire
Monday 12th June	Carlton Ballroom, Slough, Berkshire
Saturday 17 June	Essoldo, Slough, Berkshire
Sunday 18th June	Community Centre, Southall, Middlesex
Wednesday 21st June	Carlton Ballroom, Slough, Berkshire
Saturday 24th June	Rugby Football Ground, Twickenham (open air concert)
Monday 26th June	Carlton Ballroom, Slough, Berkshire
Wednesday 28th June	Carlton Ballroom, Slough, Berkshire
Sunday 2nd July	Community Centre, Southall, Middlesex
Wednesday 5th July	Town Hall, High Wycombe, Buckinghamshire
Saturday 8 July	Gaumont Pier, Southampton, Hampshire
Wednesday 19th July	Town Hall, High Wycombe, Buckinghamshire
Saturday 29th July	Essoldo, Slough, Berkshire
Sunday 30th July	Carlton Ballroom, Slough, Berkshire
Tuesday 1st August	Walton Hop, Walton-on-Thames, Surrey
Wednesday 2nd August	Carlton Ballroom, Slough, Berkshire
Saturday 5th August	Southampton Pier, Southampton, Hampshire
Monday 7th August	Carlton Ballroom, Slough, Berkshire
Sunday 13th August	Carlton Ballroom, Slough, Berkshire
Wednesday 16th August	Town Hall, High Wycombe, Buckinghamshire
Saturday 19th August	Gaumont, Southampton, Hampshire (morning)
Saturday 19th August	Southampton Pier, Southampton, Hampshire (evening)
Saturday 2nd September	Agincourt Ballroom, Camberley, Surrey
Sunday 3rd September	Community Centre, Southall, Middlesex
Saturday 9th September	Mental Hospital, Basingstoke, Hampshire

Quite extraordinary to think that The Jaywalkers performed at a hospital for the mentally ill, but it is probably put into perspective by virtue of the fact that they were the support act for Screaming Lord Sutch & The Savages at this particular gig!

Only five days earlier at a gig in Reading the Berkshire Chronicle reported, "he (Sutch) wears his hair about 18 inches long and always appears in odd clothes like an old tattered loin cloth or some Eskimo outfit".

Sutch was obviously familiar with Blackmore from his audition but one wonders whether Sutch watched the shy 16-year old perform at this gig?

Wednesday 13th September	Carlton Ballroom, Slough, Berkshire
Saturday 23rd September	Essoldo, Slough, Berkshire
Wednesday 27th September	Decca Studios, West Hampstead, North London

This was the date of Blackmore's first ever professional recording session in the morning at Decca's Studio in Broadhurst Gardens, West Hampstead. According to Blackmore it was done as a demo with the hope that, if good enough, Decca Records would have signed the band up.

The two songs were 'Stolen Hours' and 'My Blue Heaven'. The latter was an old song written in 1927 by Walter Donaldson and George A. Whiting and originally recorded that year by Gene Austin, although it's more than likely that they chose to perform it based on Fats Domino's more up-tempo version released in 1956. 'Stolen Hours' had been written especially for them. Blackmore told the author in 1998, "it was awful." Decca did nothing more with it and presumably the tapes are still sitting in the archives somewhere.

Wednesday 27th September	Carlton Ballroom, Slough, Berkshire

Following on from the morning session at Decca, it was back to gigging in the evening.

Saturday 30th September	Town Hall, Staines, Middlesex
Sunday 1st October	Community Centre, Southall, Middlesex

Wednesday 4th October	Carlton Ballroom, Slough, Berkshire
Thursday 5th October	Crown Ballroom, Banbury, Oxfordshire
Saturday 14th October	Agincourt Ballroom, Camberley, Surrey
Sunday 15th October	Carlton Ballroom, Slough, Berkshire
Saturday 21st October	Essoldo, Slough, Berkshire
Tuesday 24th October	Walton Hop, Walton-on-Thames, Surrey
Saturday 28th October	Gaumont, Southampton, Hampshire (morning gig)
Saturday 28th October	Southampton Pier, Southampton, Hampshire (evening gig)
Wednesday 1st November	Carlton Ballroom, Slough, Berkshire
Saturday 4th November	Park Ballroom, Southampton, Southampton, Hampshire
Tuesday 7th November	Walton Hop, Walton-on-Thames, Surrey
Wednesday 8th November	Agincourt Ballroom, Camberley, Surrey
Friday 17th November	USAF, Bushy Park, Middlesex
Monday 20th November	Granada, Dartford, Essex (two shows)

This gig was a last-minute replacement for Shirley Douglas on a package tour headlined by Billy Fury & Eden Kane. The matinee show started at 6:40pm and the evening show at 8:50pm.

Tuesday 21st November	Guildhall, Portsmouth, Hampshire (two shows)

The bands' stint on a bill with the great Billy Fury was over almost as soon as it started, with this second show as Douglas returned for the rest of the tour.

Friday 24th November	Essoldo, Paddington
Saturday 25th November	Starlight Ballroom (?), Crawley, West Sussex
Sunday 26th November	Community Centre, Southall, Middlesex

Supporting Gene Vincent. Blackmore's first encounter with the mercurial and unpredictable American rocker.

Wednesday 29th November	Adelphi, Slough, Berkshire
Thursday 30th November	Agincourt Ballroom, Camberley, Surrey
Sunday 10th December	Carlton Ballroom, Slough, Berkshire

This was the band's last gig of the year. There was undoubtedly more gigs in early 1962 but I have not been able to unearth these yet. The forgotten bands website claims that in the winter of 1961 Terry Maybey was hospitalised and Derek "Degsy" Sirmon (who was just 15 at the time), drummer with The Conchords, got asked to step in which gave him a regular job with them although it is was only briefly until Maybey was fit to return.

April-May 1962 – The Condors

Mike Dee - vocals
Ritchie Blackmore - guitar
Terry Mabey - drums
David Tippler - bass
Brian Mansell - rhythm guitar

It won't take much to deduce that this is exactly the same band as Mike Dee & The Jaywalkers. The band decided to change names to avoid confusion with Peter Jay & The Jaywalkers and picked The Condors. Unbeknown to them it resulted in a similar situation but this time it worked in their favour. They soon discovered there was another band called The Condors who backed Johnny Milton and it was actually that band that the George Cooper Organisation wanted. The Jaywalkers had previously been with the Cooper agency but had been dropped and switched to the Rudy Stanton Agency but seemingly in the confusion were booked for a twenty-three-date package tour headlined by the American artists Johnny Burnette, Gary "US" Bonds and Gene McDaniel.

The bill was also completed with the all-vocal group, The Kestrels; Danny Rivers and Mark Wynter, all of whom The Condors were employed to back on the tour. Because they were used in a backing capacity only it did mean that lead singer Mike Dee wasn't required with the other acts although they did get to open the show with their own spot, which probably consisted of two songs maximum.

As in keeping with the package tour format of the time, two shows were performed at each venue — a matinee show and an evening show. For overseas readers perhaps mystified that so many of the venues have the same name, the Granada was a cinema chain that also doubled up as concert venues. In all, forty-six shows in twenty-three days!

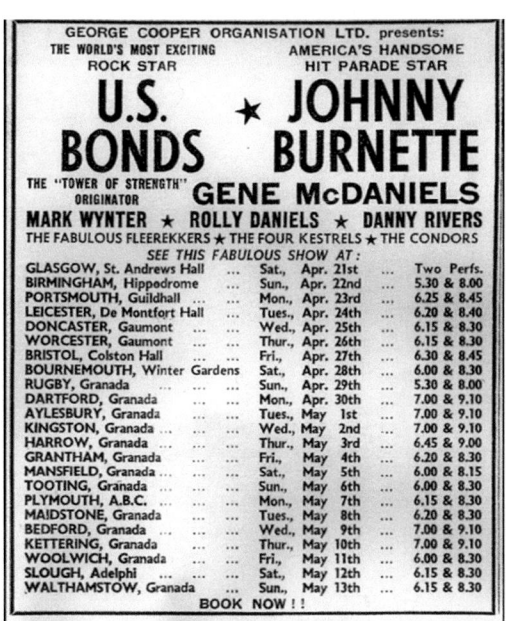

1962

Date	Venue
Saturday 21st April	St Andrew's Hall, Glasgow
Sunday 22nd April	Hippodrome, Birmingham, Warwickshire
Monday 23rd April	Guildhall, Portsmouth, Hampshire
Tuesday 24th April	De Montfort Hall, Leicester, Leicestershire
Wednesday 25th April	Gaumont, Doncaster, South Yorkshire
Thursday 26th April	Gaumont, Worcester, Worcestershire
Friday 27th April	Colston Hall, Bristol, Gloucestershire
Saturday 28th April	Winter Gardens, Bournemouth, Dorset
Sunday 29th April	Granada, Rugby, Warwickshire

Monday 30th April	Granada, Dartford, Essex
Tuesday 1st May	Granada, Aylesbury, Buckinghamshire
Wednesday 2nd May	Granada, Kingston, Surrey
Thursday 3rd May	Granada Harrow, Middlesex
Friday 4th May	Granada, Grantham, Lincolnshire
Saturday 5th May	Granada, Mansfield, Nottinghamshire
Sunday 6th May	Granada, Tooting, London
Monday 7th May	ABC, Plymouth, Devon
Tuesday 8th May	Granada, Maidstone, Kent
Wednesday 9th May	Granada, Bedford, Bedfordshire

The local paper report for this show was that the Granada was by no means full. However, The Kestrals and Danny Rivers, backed by The Condors both went down well.

Thursday 10th May	Granada, Kettering, Northamptonshire
Friday 11th May	Granada, Woolwich, London
Saturday 12th May	Granada, Slough, Berkshire
Sunday 13th May	Granada, Walthamstow, London

Despite such a full-on tour The Condors called it a day straight after the tour finished. Sutch had been eying up Blackmore, perhaps regretting not taking him the previous year, but this time Ritchie got the gig with one of the busiest bands in the country.

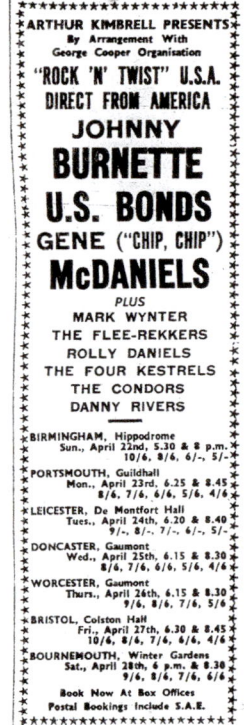

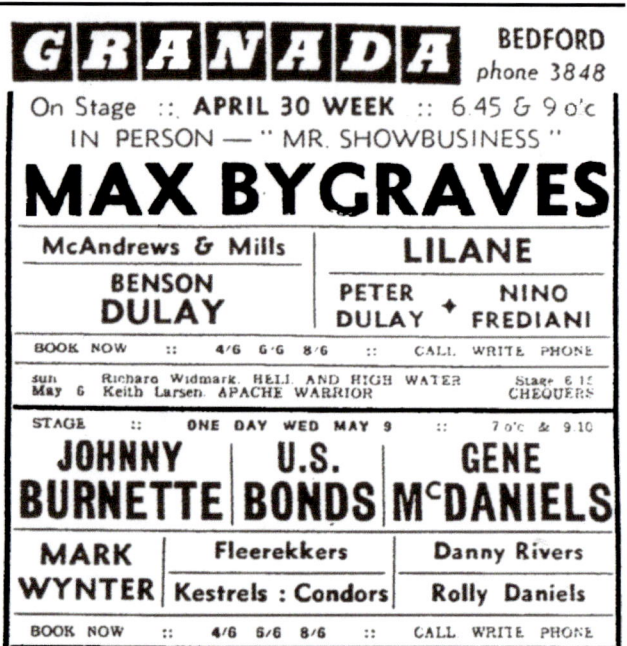

May-12th October 1962 – Screaming Lord Sutch & The Savages

David Sutch - vocals
Ritchie Blackmore - guitar
Carlo Little - drums
Ricky Brown - bass
Andy Wren - piano (replaced by Freddie 'Fingers' Lee)

Although Blackmore's first professional stint with The Jaywalkers had paid reasonably well and helped to hone his skills, joining The Savages was a major leap forward. Sutch, despite being a poor vocalist, made up for it as a performer and always ensured he had top notch musicians backing him. Although renowned as a "penny pincher" Sutch also paid better than most bands of this stature and Blackmore's usual gig fee during this stint was £4 per night.

It is unclear exactly what Blackmore's first show was, but I have listed them from the first possible date that he could have played. The vast majority of the gigs listed here come from Carlo Little's gig diary as published on his website, alas, the actual venues were not included.

1962

Date	Venue
Tuesday 15th May	Wallington, Surrey
Friday 18th May	Peckham, London
Saturday 19th May	Chelmsford, Essex
Sunday 20th May	Hayes, Middlesex
Monday 21st May	South Norwood, London
Thursday 24th May	New Brighton, Cheshire
Saturday 26th May	Bletchley, Buckinghamshire
Thursday 31st May	Rushden, Northamptonshire
Friday 1st June	Waltham Abbey, Essex
Saturday 2nd June	Corn Exchange, Peterborough, Northamptonshire

Supported by The Escorts.

Wednesday 6th June	Catford, London
Friday 8th June	Gravesend, Kent
Saturday 9th June	Subscription Rooms, Stroud, Gloucestershire
Monday 11th June	Hayes, Middlesex

First of two gigs in one night!

Monday 11th June	California Ballroom, Dunstable, Bedfordshire

Second gig of the night. Shows at the California were known to finish late. It also had two stages at each end of the ballroom, so that the music could be continuous. Also on the bill were the Ray Miller Orchestra and Jeff Knight and the Challengers.

Tuesday 12th June	Kilburn, London
Friday 15th June	Doncaster, South Yorkshire
Saturday 16th June	Doncaster, South Yorkshire
Sunday 17th June	Doncaster, South Yorkshire

Sutch and The Savages is probably the only band in history to have done a three-night tour of Doncaster! One of these shows was at Yarborough Social Club, the other venues are unknown.

Friday 22nd June	Winchester, Hampshire
Saturday 23rd June	Barnehurst, London
Sunday 24th June	Hackney, London
Monday 25th June	Town Hall, Wembley, London

Sutch and his band were supported by Paul Dean & the Dreamers, a local outfit fronted by future acting star and Savage Paul Nicholas. That night, it was so crowded that many of the girls stood on the bench seats around the hall perimeters to see the band properly and promptly punctured the leather with their stiletto heels, causing a mild furore that made the local papers. After the gig a young Keith Moon, who was drummer in a local band called Lee Stuart & the Escorts, approached Carlo Little to ask him for drum lessons.

Wednesday 27th June	Maida Vale, London
Thursday 28th June	Queens Hall, Barnstaple, Devon
Friday 29th June	Town Hall, Torquay, Devon
Saturday 30th June	Civic Hall, Exeter, Devon

Sunday 1st July	unknown venue
Monday 2nd July	unknown venue
Friday 6th July	Harrow, Middlesex
Saturday 7th July	Southampton, Hampshire
Sunday 8th July	Littlehampton, West Sussex

First of two gigs in one night.

Sunday 8th July	Worthing, West Sussex

Second gig of the night.

Friday 13th July	Epsom, Surrey
Saturday 14th July	Chippenham, Wiltshire
Monday 16th July	Burton upon Trent, Staffordshire
Wednesday 18th July	Kidderminster, Worcestershire
Thursday 19th July	Mayfield, East Sussex

Mayfield is a village. Sutch would play anywhere as long as the money was good enough.

Friday 20th July	Ely, Cambridgeshire
Saturday 21st July	Skegness, Lincolnshire
Sunday 22nd July	Doncaster, South Yorkshire
Monday 23rd July	Fleetwood, Lancashire
Wednesday 25th July	Sevenoaks, Kent
Friday 27th July	Gosport, Hampshire
Saturday 28th July	Stafford, Staffordshire
Thursday 2nd August	Rushden, Northamptonshire
Friday 3rd August	St. Ives, Cambridgeshire
Saturday 4th August	Romford, Essex
Sunday 5th August	Community Centre, Southall, Middlesex
Tuesday 7th August	Swindon, Wiltshire
Wednesday 8th August	Crawley, West Sussex
Friday 10th August	Edmonton, London
Saturday 11th August	Wisbech, Cambridgeshire
Wednesday 15th August	Northampton, Northamptonshire
Thursday 16th August	Conservative Club, Bedford, Bedfordshire

Also on the bill were Duke D'Mond and the Barron Knights. The local press advert for this show billed Sutch as appearing in person "direct from the nuthouse". Given that the previous year, he had played a show in a mental hospital, when Blackmore supported as part of The Jaywalkers, the advertising was relatively accurate!

Friday 17th August	Town Hall, Buckingham, Buckinghamshire

Supported by The Senators.

Saturday 18th August	Memorial Hall, Northwich, Cheshire
Tuesday 28th August	Wallington, Surrey
Friday 31st August	Kingston, Surrey
Saturday 1st September	Redhill, Surrey
Sunday 2nd September	Manchester, Lancashire
Monday 3rd September	Manchester, Lancashire
Tuesday 4th September	Manchester, Lancashire
Wednesday 5th September	Manchester, Lancashire
Thursday 6th September	Manchester, Lancashire
Friday 7th September	Manchester, Lancashire
Saturday 8th September	Manchester, Lancashire

Different venues (unknown) were played nightly during this Manchester tour.

Monday 10th September	Portsmouth, Hampshire
Tuesday 11th September	Greenwich, London
Wednesday 12th September	Cardiff, Glamorgan
Saturday 15th September	Floral Hall, Morecambe, Lancashire

Also on the bill was The Atlantics. Their drummer Neil Newsome recalled, "I remember standing in awe in front of Ritchie. Even without our band we would go and see them. I've always revered him. You can't take it away from the other guitarists but he's always been my firm favourite. He sat down on his amp with his guitar and Billy Clarke (Atlantics guitarist) sat down and he was showing Billy harmonics. He played a number called 'Czardas', like a Russian type speeding up thing and the speed on the guitar was phenomenal. He just sat there and played it ad-lib with Billy. We just stood with our mouths open. Bear in mind he was only seventeen years old then."

Monday 17th September	Leyton, London
Wednesday 19th September	Leyton Buzzard, Bedfordshire
Friday 21st September	Thorne, South Yorkshire
Saturday 22nd September	Ramsey, Huntingdonshire
Sunday 23rd September	Hull, East Riding
Tuesday 25th September	East Grinstead, West Sussex
Wednesday 26th September	Barnet, Hertfordshire
Friday 28th September	Gosport, Hampshire
Saturday 29th September	Oxford, Oxfordshire
Sunday 30th September	Castleford, West Yorkshire
Monday 31st September	Kidderminster, Worcestershire
Wednesday 2nd October	Esham, Surrey
Thursday 3rd October	Watford, Hertfordshire
Friday 4th October	Reading, Berkshire
Saturday 5th October	Epsom, Surrey
Sunday 6th October	Northampton, Northamptonshire
Monday 7th October	Chatham, Kent
Wednesday 9th October	Toton, Nottinghamshire
Thursday 10th October	Sevenoaks, Kent
Friday 11th October	Lydney, Gloucestershire
Saturday 12th October	Putney, London

This was Blackmore's last gig with Sutch.

October 1962-April 1964 – The Outlaws

Ritchie Blackmore - lead guitar
Ken Lundgren - rhythm guitar
Chas Hodges - bass, vocals
Mick Underwood - drums

The Outlaws drummer Don Groom left to tour with Buddy Holly's band The Crickets, and around the same time guitarist Lorne Greene left for pastures new. Mick Underwood had already got the job to replace Groom and evidently auditions were held at the 2Is Coffee Bar in Soho. Underwood suggested Blackmore as the guitarist and he was offered the gig.

As Blackmore said to Jon Tobler in 1982, "Joe Meek said, 'how about joining my band The Outlaws?' So I said 'okay it sounds good to me.' The Outlaws were more well-known than The Savages so I was quite pleased."

Indeed The Outlaws, in-house band for independent record producer Joe Meek, were far more established than Sutch. They had already released several records — five singles under their own name, and others backing Mike Berry. They had also released an album, *Dream Of The West*, the previous year. In addition to that Meek used them as the backing band for several of his other artists and as such it guaranteed Blackmore income from both studio sessions and live gigs.

Although it was common place to do a studio session in the morning then jump in the van and drive to a town for a gig that evening, because of the haphazard nature of studio sessions and live work, even though Blackmore was kept extremely busy thanks to Meek's relentless work schedule, documenting the gigs accurately can be tricky and several of the dates listed here are unconfirmed.

1962

Date   **Venue**

Tuesday 16th October   Town Hall, Cheltenham, Gloucestershire

Four days earlier Blackmore did his last gig with Sutch. It is not certain when he did his first show with The Outlaws. Although it is documented that Groom had left to join The Crickets tour, that did not start until 2nd November, and I have not been able to ascertain exactly when in October the changeover with Underwood and Blackmore occurred as The Outlaws continued as Mike Berry's backing band through the line-up change. If Blackmore did perform at this show, then it would have been an interesting gig as his previous employer was also on the bill.

Wednesday 17th October   Eel Pie Island Hotel, Twickenham
This gig was also a double bill with Sutch & The Savages.

Friday 26th October   Public Hall, Preston, Lancashire
This was another gig The Outlaws did backing Mike Berry and Blackmore almost certainly did this one. Support came from the Syd Munson Orchestra and that well-known beat combo from Liverpool called The Beatles.

I have yet to unearth any other shows for 1962. The Outlaws were also recording during this period though.

Friday 7th December   The Chaps - Poppin' Part I / Poppin' Part II (Parlophone R4979)

Not a gig but a notable date for Blackmore as it was the first release to feature his guitar playing. This instrumental medley consisted of three numbers on each side. On side A, 'Return To Sender', 'Next Door To An Angel' and 'Bobby's Girl'. On the B-side, 'It Might As Well Rain Until September', 'Ramblin Rose' and 'Telstar'.

Because of his association with Meek, some information over the years has claimed that Blackmore plays on the number one hit 'Telstar' by the Tornados and the confusion might have been partly caused by his performance on this version.

The Chaps was just a pseudonym that Meek gave The Outlaws for this release.

In February '63 Mike Berry told the press that he had stopped working with The Outlaws but when he was announced as being part of the, then forthcoming Brenda Lee tour, The Outlaws remained as Berry's backing group. This was also the biggest tour that Blackmore had performed up until that point. Although The Condors tour had seem them playing at many of the big cinemas, the Brenda Lee tour included several venues that will be familiar with Purple and Rainbow fans.

At some of the gigs Bert Weedon performed instead of Mike Berry but the programmes show that The Outlaws opened the shows with their own set anyway.

Further evidence that they performed at the shows that Mike Berry didn't play at was documented in *Black Knight* from my interview with Ken Lundgren who recalled 17 year old Blackmore's encounter with the 42 year old Weedon: "One time we were on a package show, and it included Bert Weedon. Bert and Ritchie were on the stage when we were doing our soundcheck and of course Bert was showing off doing a finger style version of something, 'Etude in E' that most guitarists play to show they know what they are doing. Ritchie watched him for a couple of seconds and launched into 'Flight Of The Bumble Bee' just to bowl over Bert Weedon who'd had a number one hit at the time, and was a good player. But Ritchie was of that nature, here comes Bert Weedon who is really famous and I'm going to knock him over and he did it almost maliciously in a sort of Ritchie Blackmore good-natured way. The rest of us were standing there going "come on Ritchie leave it out" because there was no need for that. Everybody knew how fast Ritchie was but he wanted to put it in people's faces."

1963

Date	Venue
Monday 11th March	Capitol, Cardiff, Glamorgan
Tuesday 12th March	Gaumont, Worcester, Worcestershire
Wednesday 13th March	Hippodrome, Brighton, East Sussex
Thursday 14th March	Granada, Harrow, Middlesex
Friday 15th March	Granada, Woolwich, London
Saturday 16th March	Granada, Walthamstow, London
Sunday 17th March	City Hall, Newcastle, Northumberland
Monday 18th March	City Hall, Sheffield, South Yorkshire
Tuesday 19th March	Odeon, Liverpool, Lancashire
Wednesday 20th March	Town Hall, Birmingham, Warwickshire
Thursday 21st March	Colston Hall, Bristol, Gloucestershire
Friday 22nd March	Granada, Kingston, Surrey
Saturday 23rd March	Adelphi, Slough, Berkshire
Sunday 24th March	Theatre, Coventry, Warwickshire
Monday 25th March	Guildhall, Portsmouth, Hampshire
Tuesday 26th March	Kings Hall, Belfast, Northern Ireland
Wednesday 27th March	National Stadium, Dublin, Southern Ireland
Thursday 28th March	Savoy Theatre, Cork, Southern Ireland
Friday 29th March	Odeon, Manchester, Lancashire
Saturday 30th March	Winter Gardens, Bournemouth, Dorset
Sunday 31st March	Granada, Tooting, London

This concluded the Brenda Lee tour. It is not clear which of the shows Mike Berry appeared at, backed by The Outlaws and which shows Bert Weedon appeared at.

The Outlaws were signed to the Galaxy Entertainment Agency which included amongst its roster, American rock 'n' roll star Gene Vincent. This would appear to have been the link to their next gigs. In the sixties the musicians union had a lot more clout than it does today and with regards to overseas artists the MU's objective was to give work to UK musicians backing the American artists rather than just accepting that they came to the UK with their own touring bands. Although in the case of Gene Vincent he had already encountered problems with the MU in America. A dispute with the US tax authorities and the American Musicians' Union over payments to his band and his having sold the band's equipment to pay a tax bill led Vincent to leave the United States for Europe in the late fifties.

On 16th April 1960, during a UK tour, along with Eddie Cochran and the songwriter Sharon Sheeley Vincent was involved in a high-speed traffic accident in a private-hire cab in Chippenham, Wiltshire. He survived although Cochran, who had been thrown from the vehicle, suffered serious brain injuries and died the next day. Vincent returned to the United States after the accident, but promoter Don Arden arranged for Vincent to return to the UK for an extensive tour in 1961. After the tour's overwhelming success, Vincent moved to Britain in 1963. He had used various backing bands before settling on Sounds Incorporated in early 1961, although, when not available, other bands were also used from time to time.

In late '62 The Echoes was backing him and by early '63 The Jokers. With a constant changing of "pick up" bands, it makes it very difficult to establish exactly who backed him at each gig.

Ian Wallis is a noted archivist of US rock 'n' roll stars UK tours and has published two books chronicling it all from the fifties. Although even he is uncertain about all of them. Concerning Vincent's gigs in March '63 Wallis often lists the backing band as either The Jokers or The Outlaws, obviously oblivious to the fact that The Outlaws were on the Brenda Lee Tour.

The gigs that follow is an attempt to document the gigs The Outlaws did with Vincent. Working on Wallis' data, when he is uncertain whether or not it was The Jokers or The Outlaws are listed in grey although as far as Wallis is concerned both bands continued to back Vincent up to June, interchanging with alarming regularity.

1963

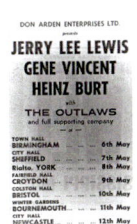

Date	Venue
Wednesday 3rd April	400 Ballroom, Torquay, Devon
Thursday 4th April	Majestic, Plymouth, Devon
Friday 5th April	Flamingo, Redruth, Cornwall
Thursday 11th April	Hippodrome, Bristol, Gloucestershire

Although Wallis has question marks over these gigs as to who backed Vincent, particularly Plymouth and Redruth, it seems logical that it would have been The Outlaws, having done the first show in Torquay.

Sunday 5th May	Broadway, Letchworth, Hertfordshire

Two performances.

Monday 6th May	Pinewood Studios, Ivor Heath, Buckinghamshire

The outlaws spent the morning filming 'Law & Order' atop of scaffolding for the film Live It Up! *As soon as the filming was over they were off in the van to Birmingham for the start of a prestigious tour, backing former Tornado Heinz Burt and another US rock 'n' roll great, Jerry Lee Lewis. A perfect example of the MU's impact, pairing up a US touring musician with a UK band although Lewis brought with him his drummer, Morris Tarrant, so Mick Underwood had to sit out that part of the show. Gene Vincent completed the bill but was backed by The Jokers, although they were credited as The Blue Caps. Surely it would have made sense to have the one backing band? The Outlaws did get to do their own set to open the second half of show however and they also got featured in the tour programme. There were two performances per night.*

Date	Venue
Monday 6th May	Town Hall, Birmingham, Warwickshire
Tuesday 7th May	City Hall, Sheffield, South Yorkshire
Wednesday 8th May	Rialto Theatre, York, North Yorkshire
Thursday 9th May	Fairfield Halls, Croydon, Surrey
Friday 10th May	Colston Hall, Bristol, Gloucestershire

Saturday 11th May	Winter Gardens, Bournemouth, Dorset
Sunday 12th May	City Hall, Newcastle, Northumberland

This brief UK tour was followed immediately with a week's residency with Jerry Lee Lewis at the Star Club in Hamburg, and Blackmore's first visit to Germany.

Monday 13th May	Star Club, Hamburg, Germany
Wednesday 15th May	Star Club, Hamburg, Germany
Thursday 16th May	Star Club, Hamburg, Germany
Friday 17th May	Star Club, Hamburg, Germany
Saturday 18th May	Star Club, Hamburg, Germany
Sunday 19th May	Star Club, Hamburg, Germany
May	various US military bases, Germany

Other shows backing Jerry Lee Lewis were done in Germany but dates and venues unknown. Outlaws continued touring with Lewis until 5th June.

Monday 27th May	The Pavilion, Bath, Somerset

Some sources say the venue was Theatre Royal which Wallis credits as the Royal Hall. Screaming Lord Sutch And The Savages and Rod Starr And The Stereos were also on the bill.

Tuesday 28th May	Public Hall, Wallington, Surrey

A three-band bill that included Tommy Bruce & The Bruisers and The Alphabeats. Despite being the top name on the bill Jerry Lee Lewis took to the stage early because it was the first of two gigs that evening. Keith Temple of The Alphabeats (misspelled as 'The Alpha Beats') recollects about the show, "The Outlaws probably did 15 minutes or so on their own before Jerry Lee Lewis appeared onstage. The Outlaws backed him from 8:15 to 9:15pm. Tommy Bruce and The Bruisers would probably do an hour from 9:15 to 10:15pm, and we probably finished off the evening until 11pm."

Tuesday 28th May	Ballroom, East Grinstead, West Sussex

Second gig of the day.

Wednesday 29th May	Plaza, Birmingham, Warwickshire

The first of two gigs that day.

Wednesday 29th May	Ritz Dance & Social Club, Birmingham, Warwickshire

Second gig of the day.

Thursday 30th May	Matrix Hall, Coventry, Warwickshire
Friday 31st May	King's Hall, Stoke-on-Trent, Staffordshire
Saturday 1st June	M.V Royal Daffodil, English Channel

This was a Channel Crossing trip from Southend-on-Sea to France for English fans to watch a concert in Boulogne headlined by Jerry Lee Lewis and including several other acts including Nero & The Gladiators and Ricky Vallance. The ferry departed Southend at 9:00am and on the journey The Outlaws performed their own set on board the ferry. Probably the only gig Blackmore has ever done off land!

Saturday 1st June	Le Guitar Club Casino, Boulogne, France

On board the MV Royal Daffodil with memebrs of The Atlantics. The Outlaws performed on the way to Boulogne. Left to right: Mick Underwood, Billy Clarke, Ritchie, his girlfriend Jacqui Shirley, Jamie Lee & Barry Taylor.

After backing Jerry Lee, all the fans and artists returned to Southend arriving back at 9:30pm.

Sunday 2nd June — Empire Theatre, Liverpool, Lancashire

A long journey from Southend to Liverpool, and then straight back to France again the following evening! According to both Derek Henderson the author of Gene Vincent: A Companion who runs the Gene Vincent website spentbrothers.com, as well as Ian Wallis, this gig was a double bill with Gene Vincent, with Wallis stating that The Outlaws backed both artists.

Monday 3rd June — L'Olympia Bruno Coquatrix, Paris, France

Three songs from this concert were broadcasted on French Radio: 'You Win Again', 'Your Cheatin' Heart' and 'Good Golly Miss Molly'. This recording has subsequently been bootlegged and is the earliest known live recording to feature Blackmore. Some sources claim there was a second show in Paris on the 5th but Lewis was back in the States by then.

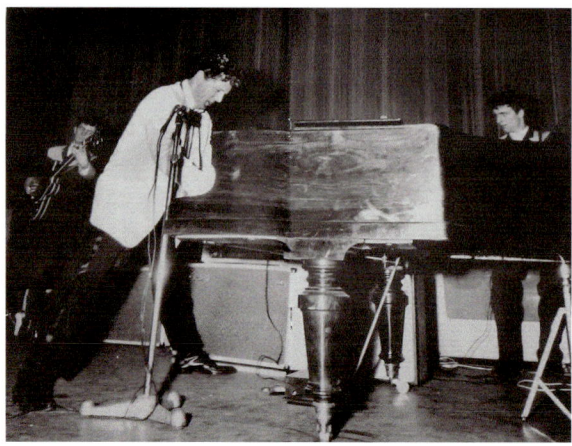

Left: With Gene Vincent at the Star Club, Hamburg. Right: Performing at the Olympia in Paris with Jerry Lee Lewis. Recorded for radio, the earliest known live recording to feature Ritchie.

The Outlaws resumed live work with Gene Vincent that saw them through to the end of the year but once again, some dates are unconfirmed as including The Outlaws and could have possibly been with The Jokers.

Thursday 6th June	Queens Hall, Barnstaple, Devon
Friday 7th June	Town Hall, Torquay, Devon
Saturday 8th June	Civic Hall, Exeter, Devon
Tuesday 18th June	McKilroys, Swindon, Wiltshire
Friday 21st June	Ritz Dance & Social Club, Birmingham, Warwickshire
Thursday 27th June	Locarno, Liverpool, Lancashire
Friday 28th June	Gravesend, Kent **UNCONFIRMED**
Saturday 29th June	Wilton Hall, Bletchley, Buckinghamshire **UNCONFIRMED**

Both of the above shows were mentioned in the music press but possibly got cancelled.

Monday 1st July	Ferneham Hall, Fareham, Hampshire
Friday 5th July	Alexandra Palace, Wood Green, London
Saturday 6th July	BBC Studios, Charing Cross, London

BBC Radio session for Saturday Club. The Outlaws recorded five numbers with Vincent: 'High Blood Pressure', 'Baby Blue', 'Bluejean Bop', 'Crazy Beat' and 'Lotta Lovin''. The show was broadcasted on 20th July.

Sunday 7th July — Odeon Theatre, Weston-super-Mare, Somerset

Two performances in Ritchie's birth town.

Friday 12th July — Music Hall, Shrewsbury, Shropshire

Almost certainly on this day, although possibly the day before, Blackmore was up to his usual prank of throwing bags of flour at people from the van. However, on this occasion he was caught in the act.

Sunday 14th July	Odeon, Southend-on-Sea, Essex
Friday 19th July	Ritz, Llanelly, Monmouthshire
Saturday 13th July	Memorial Hall, Northwich, Cheshire

Sunday 21st July	Odeon, Llandudno, Caernarfonshire
Friday 26th July	Whitehall, East Grinstead, West Sussex
Saturday 27th July	Pavilion Gardens, Buxton, Derbyshire
Saturday 27th July	Bingley Hall, Birmingham, Warwickshire
Sunday 28th July	Floral Hall, Southport, Lancashire
Saturday 10th August	California Ballroom, Dunstable, Bedfordshire
Sunday 11th August	Odeon, Folkestone, Kent
Sunday 18th August	ABC, Blackpool, Lancashire
Monday 19th August	Grand Theatre, Wolverhampton, Staffordshire

The first of six nights in a variety show backing Gene Vincent. Other acts on the bill included singer Billy Fontayne, trumpet player Nat Gonella and compere Kenny Cantor.

Tuesday 20th August	Grand Theatre, Wolverhampton, Staffordshire
Wednesday 21st August	Grand Theatre, Wolverhampton, Staffordshire
Thursday 22nd August	Grand Theatre, Wolverhampton, Staffordshire
Friday 23rd August	Grand Theatre, Wolverhampton, Staffordshire
Saturday 24th August	Cliff & Halifax, Wolverhampton, Staffordshire

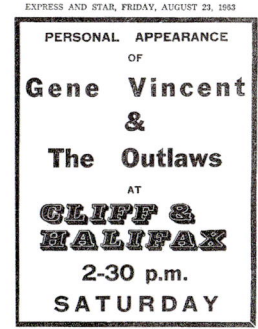

During the day the band made a personal appearance at the local electrical store signing autographs before the last show of the week. The short-lived London newspaper Sunday Citizen had picked up on the news that Blackmore had received a summons to appear at Shrewsbury Magistrates and interviewed him during his time in Wolverhampton.

Saturday 24th August	Grand Theatre, Wolverhampton, Staffordshire
Sunday 25th August	ABC, Great Yarmouth, Norfolk
Tuesday 27th August	Marine, Southport, Lancashire
Saturday 31st August	Palais, Wimbledon, London
Sunday 1st September	Odeon, Llandudno, Caernarfonshire
Monday 2nd September	Odeon, Sunderland, County Durham
Tuesday 3rd September	Imperial, Waltham Cross, Hertfordshire
Friday 6th September	Winter Gardens, Banbury, Oxfordshire
Saturday 7th September	Rink, Swadlincote, Derbyshire
Sunday 8th September	Gaumont, Bournemouth, Dorset
Monday 9th September	Magistrates Court, Shrewsbury, Shropshire

This was the day of Blackmore's hearing for depositing litter.

Friday 13th September	Town Hall, Pwllheli, Caernarfonshire
Sunday 15th September	Top Hat, Manchester, Lancashire
Monday 16th September	Star Club, Hamburg, Germany

First night of a weeks' residency.

Tuesday 17th September	Star Club, Hamburg, Germany
Wednesday 18th September	Star Club, Hamburg, Germany
Thursday 19th September	Star Club, Hamburg, Germany

Friday 20th September — Star Club, Hamburg, Germany
During this week Ritchie met Margit Volkmar. In the words of Mick Underwood "he was besotted with her."

Monday 23rd September — BBC Studios, Charing Cross, London
BBC Radio session for Saturday Club. The Outlaws recorded six numbers with Vincent: 'Rip It Up', 'Frankie And Johnny', 'Crazy Beat', 'Another Saturday Night', I'm Gonna Catch Me A Rat', 'Long Tall Sally' and 'Dance To The Bop'.

Thursday 26th September — City Hall, Salisbury, Wiltshire
Saturday 28th September — Pier, Hastings, East Sussex
On the day of this show the Saturday Club performance recorded five days earlier was broadcasted by BBC Radio.

Sunday 29th September — Princess Theatre Club, Manchester, Lancashire
Monday 30th September — Pavilion, Bath, Somerset
Tuesday 1st October — Public Hall, Wallington, Surrey
Wednesday 2nd October — Town Hall, Stourbridge, Worcestershire
Thursday 3rd October — Town Hall, Kidderminster, Worcestershire
Monday 7th October — New Majestic, Eccles, Lancashire
Saturday 19th October — Boom Boom, Belfast, Northern Ireland
Sunday 20th October — Boom Boom, Belfast, Northern Ireland
Monday 21st October — Boom Boom, Belfast, Northern Ireland

The above four dates were listed in the music press but probably didn't take place. Back in June the music press had also run a report that The Outlaws had signed as Gene's "regular accompanying unit" and that they would tour France in October backing him. Vincent's French (and Belgian) tour commenced on the 4th and ran through to the 31st but The Outlaws did not back him. For that tour he was backed by a French group, The Sunlights. Gene Vincent continued touring the UK to the end of the year. Although The Outlaws definitely backed him at the last gig of the year, it is not a certainty that they backed at all the shows, but all of Vincent's documented gigs through to the end of December are included regardless. Hopefully one day I will be able to clarify which shows were with The Outlaws.

Saturday 9th November — St Mary's Hall, Putney, London
Thursday 14th November — Granada, Kingston, Surrey*
This package tour was headlined by Duane Eddy and Little Richard. However Little Richard injured his ankle and went home before this show. Gene Vincent was the replacement at all shows marked.*

Wednesday 20th November — City Hall, Sheffield, South Yorkshire*
Thursday 21st November — Fairfield Halls, Croydon, Surrey*
Friday 22nd November — Gaumont, Lewisham, London*
Saturday 23rd November — Winter Gardens, Bournemouth, Dorset*
Sunday 24th November — De Montfort Hall, Leicester, Leicestershire*
Monday 25th November — Odeon, Luton, Bedfordshire*
Tuesday 26th November — Odeon, Liverpool, Lancashire*
Wednesday 27th November — Odeon, Leeds, West Yorkshire*
Thursday 28th November — Odeon, Manchester, Lancashire*
Friday 29th November — Odeon, Birmingham, Warwickshire*
On the day of this show the film Live It Up! was released. Ritchie's first film appearance.

Saturday 30th November — Odeon, Glasgow, Lanarkshire*
Sunday 1st December — Odeon, Sunderland, County Durham
Saturday 7th December — New Majestic, Eccles, Lancashire
Thursday 12th December — Town Hall, Birmingham, Warwickshire
Thursday 19th December — Gaumont State, Kilburn, London
Friday 20th December — Ovaltine Ballroom, Kings Langley, Hertfordshire

Monday 23rd December	Winter Gardens, Bournemouth, Dorset
Tuesday 24th December	De Montfort Hall, Leicester, Leicestershire
Saturday 28th December	California Ballroom, Dunstable, Bedfordshire

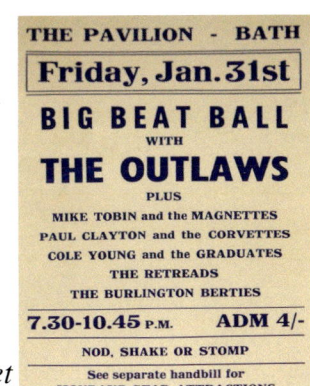

1964

Date	Venue
Friday 31st January	The Pavilion, Bath, Somerset
Wednesday 18th March	City Hall, Salisbury, Wiltshire

In the morning Ritchie and his pregnant girlfriend Margit got married at Ealing Register Office. After a reception at his parents' house, the newly married couple set off with the rest of The Outlaws to this gig as the support act for The Rolling Stones.

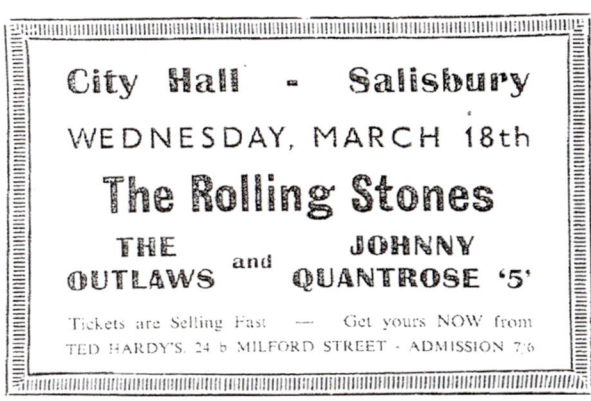

After their time backing rocker Gene Vincent came to an end in December '63, Joe Meek fixed for them to tour Ireland with his country performer Houston Wells as the replacement for Wells previous band the Marksmen. The gig data for this Irish tour that I unearthed back in 2005 was originally posted on the now defunct *More Black than Purple* website. At the time I had listed the January dates that Wells did in Ireland but further research tells me he was still with the Marksmen at that point and split with them straight after it. Thanks to Gerry Gallagher of irish-showbands.com who helped out with dates. According to Mick Underwood, it was a real come down having backed Gene Vincent and Jerry Lee Lewis and he recalls many of the gigs were in Parish Halls.

Sunday 29th March	Las Vegas Ballroom, Tuam, County Galway
Friday 3rd April	Keep A Knockin' / Shake With Me

Whilst in Ireland The Outlaws fourth single, and arguably the best was released.

Tuesday 7th April	St. MacCartan's Hall, Monaghan, County Monaghan
Wednesday 8th April	Arch Ballroom, Tallow, County Waterford
Friday 10th April	Fiesta Ballroom, Letterkenny, County Donegal
Sunday 12th April	Olympia Ballroom, Waterford, County Waterford

Given the large gaps between some of the shows listed, it is more than likely that other shows were played as well. Alas Ritchie's time with The Outlaws was coming to an end. Joe Meek had it in mind for him to lead a new backing band for Heinz.

May 1964-July 1964 – Heinz & The Wild Ones

Heinz Burt – vocals, guitar
Ritchie Blackmore - guitar
Dave Adams - keyboards
Ian Broad - drums
John Andrews - bass (soon replaced by Brian Woods)

1964

Date	Venue
Sunday 10th May	Beat City, Soho, London

The band's debut gig on the opening night of this new venue.

Date	Venue
Saturday 23rd May	St George's Hall, Hinckley, Leicestershire
Saturday 30th May	Westcliff, Ramsgate, Kent
Saturday 6th June	Pavilion, Buxton, Derbyshire
Friday 12th June	Associated-Rediffusion Television, London

Some sources claim that Heinz performed on 'Ready Steady Go!' but he is not listed on IMDb. However, even though most of the programme footage for this series no longer exists, photographic evidence (which might be from a '63 performance) shows that he mimed unaccompanied.

Sunday 14th June	Top Ten Club, Belle Vue, Manchester, Lancashire
Thursday 18th June 1964	For Teenagers Only, ATV

Another TV show appearance for Heinz, but it is unclear if The Wild Ones were included.

Saturday 27th June	Pavilion Theatre, Rhyl, Flintshire

The start of a ten-week summer season as part of a variety show with comedian Arthur Askey. They performed two shows a night, six days a week, with Sundays free. Sixty-one nights, one hundred and twenty-two shows in all!

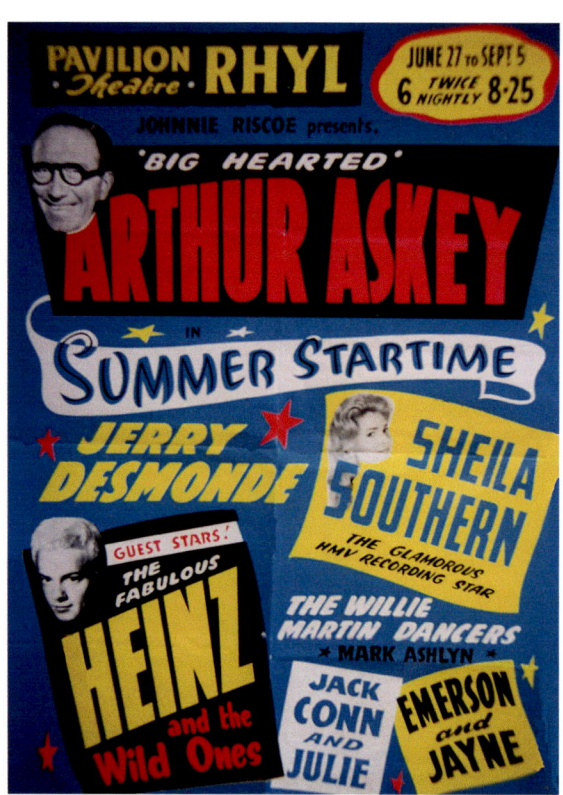

HEINZ with CHAD CHRISTIAN who penned his latest disc

HEINZ NEEDS HELP

HEINZ is in trouble! And he needs YOUR help. He urgently needs a new name for his new backing group and he reckons the best advice would come from his fans. So let's fill in the details — and then tell you about the wonderful prize he is offering.

Earlier this year, Heinz and his group the Saints amicably parted company. He signed a new outfit, the Wild Ones, to back him. But then came the trouble. There was another group of the same name . . . and they had a single released here.

So Heinz was able to keep his group's name off his new single for Decca — "Please Little Girl," though the group DID play on it. Now he has to find a brand-new moniker for the boys. Any ideas?

Says Heinz: "I've really gone from one extreme to the other . . . from the Saints to the Wild Ones. My new group is pretty wild and very exciting but we want a name that goes well with my own.

"I believe in taking advice from fans. For instance, 'Please Little Girl' was written by a fan, Chad Christian, and submitted to Joe Meek. He recorded it before Chad even knew about it! But I'm very grateful to her . . ."

And Heinz would be more than grateful for a really good group name.

Prize to the winner? An all-expenses paid trip to see Heinz in his summer season show with Arthur Askey at Rhyl, on the North Wales coast. Fares are paid, hotel, everything . . . plus theatre seats and dinner with Heinz afterwards. And you can take a friend along.

Line - up of the new group is: Burr Bailey on organ and piano — he has recorded as Dave Adams and sometimes sings as Silas Dooley Jnr. on a C & W kick; drummer is Ian Broad, who used to be with the Big Three and Freddy Starr and Midniters; on bass is new-boy John Andrews; and ex-Outlaw Ritchie Blackmore is on lead guitar.

That's it, then. Just dream up a good, original, not too way-out name for the foursome. Send it along to "Heinz" care of Record Mirror, 116 Shaftesbury Avenue, London, W.1 — and Heinz himself will be calling in to handle the judging.

PETER JONES

An extraordinary shot of Ritchie and Ian Broad during the Summer Startime "gay holiday show" in Rhyl. Ian and the 19 year-old Ritchie are pictured here with 54 year old Jack Conn (aka Doyle) a trumpeter and vocalist who was part of the variety show, along with his wife Julie.

Another photo from the same session. Left to right: Ritchie, Brian Woods, Dave Adams & Ian Broad with Heinz at the front.

Left to right: Dave Adams, Ritchie, Ian Broad & Brian Woods with Heinz seated.

July 1964-January 1965 – Heinz & The Wild Boys

Heinz Burt - vocals, guitar
Ritchie Blackmore - guitar
Dave Adams - keyboards
Ian Broad - drums (replaced by John Bednall, early December '64)
Brian Woods – bass (replaced by John Davies late '64)

During the summer season in Rhyl the band changed its name after discovering another UK band of the same name that had released a single on Fontana in May.

1964

Date **Venue**
Sunday 30th August Longleat House, Warminster, Wiltshire

Longleat House, the stately home and seat of the Marquesses of Bath was suffering financially, so Henry Frederick Thynne — the 6th Marquess of Bath, decided to open Longleat to the public in order to raise funds to maintain and preserve the house and gardens. In 1961, jazz legend Acker Bilk appeared at an outdoor concert in the grounds of the estate, but the 59-year-old Thynne was only too aware of the current craze for pop and rock 'n' roll that was captivating the nation's youth.

Sunday 3rd May 1964 saw the first in a succession of outdoor pop concerts staged at Longleat over the next two years. This show was the fourth and final concert of 1964 and was set to be by The Hollies. The 5,000 strong crowd who turned up were to be disappointed. At short notice they cancelled due to the illness of one of the band.

On a day off from performing in Rhyl, Heinz and The Wild Boys, stepped in. After the show, Lord Bath took the mic and thanked the crowd for behaving "extraordinarily well" although it was as much to do with their lack of excitement with the replacement act as anything else.

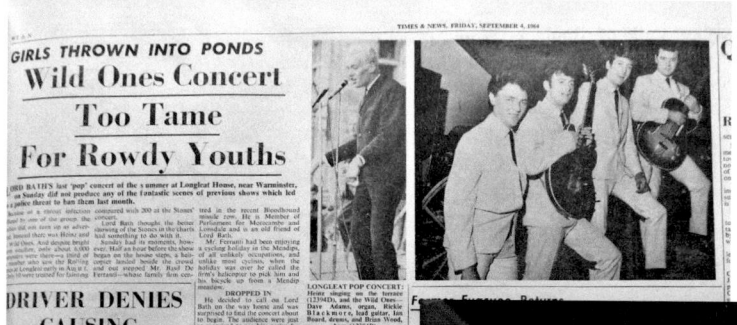

Ready to take the stage at Longleat. A welcome relief from Rhyl and Arthur Askey? Left to right: Dave Adams, Ritchie, Ian Broad, Brian Woods

Saturday 5th September — Pavilion Theatre, Rhyl, Flintshire
Last date of the summer season. What a relief!

Saturday 19th September — Torquay, Devon
Sunday 20th September — Plymouth, Devon
Sunday 27th September — ABC Alpha Studios, Aston, Birmingham, Warwickshire
Heinz performs 'Questions I Can't Answer' for Thank Your Lucky Stars. It is unclear whether or not the Wild Boys are included.

Heinz spent the first three weeks of October in Australia but the band didn't travel with him. *Thank Your Lucky Stars* was broadcasted on Saturday 3rd October. On Heinz return from Australia it was straight into a package tour billed as Your Lucky Stars with The Hollies, Dixie Cups, Jess Conrad, Tornados and Wayne Gibson.

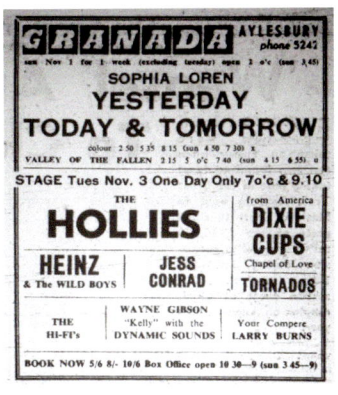

Friday 23rd October — Essoldo, Tunbridge Wells, Kent
Saturday 24th October — Theatre Royal, Norwich, Norfolk
Sunday 25th October — Regal, Boston, Lincolnshire
Monday 26th October — Rex, Haselmere, Surrey
Tuesday 27th October — Gaumont, Watford, Hertfordshire
Wednesday 28th October — ABC, Ipswich, Suffolk
Thursday 29th October — Danilo, Cannock, Staffordshire
Friday 30th October — Granada, Greenford, London CANCELLED
Friday 30th October — Palace, Douglas, Isle Of Man
Sunday 1st November — De Montfort Hall, Leicester, Leicestershire
Monday 2nd November — Granada, Dartford, Essex
Tuesday 3rd November — Granada, Aylesbury, Buckinghamshire
Wednesday 4th November — Granada, Grantham, Lincolnshire
Friday 6th November — Essoldo, Stoke on Trent, Staffordshire CANCELLED
Friday 6th November — Essoldo Huddersfield, West Yorkshire
Sunday 8th November — Theatre, Coventry, Warwickshire
Monday 16th November — The Beat Room, BBC2
TV appearance with The Wild Boys.
Tuesday 17th November — Rediffusion The Five O'Clock Club
It is unclear whether or not Heinz did this TV appearance with the band.

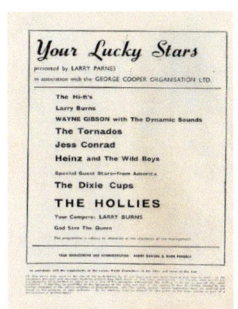

Friday 20th November — California Ballroom, Dunstable, Bedfordshire
The venue announced that "due to circumstance beyond our control Wayne Fontana and the Mindbenders will not be appearing at the California Ballroom on Friday November 20th but will be replaced by Heinz and the Wild Boys." The bill was made up with Shane and the Shane Gang and The Sneakers.

With the Summer Season show with Askey well behind him, Ritchie had to now endure a Winter Season after Harry Dawson who worked for the Cooper Organisation devised a concept of a modernised version of a pantomime built around pop stars. They spent weeks in rehearsals. A report in the Derby Evening Telegraph (12th December) said that "17-year-old John Bednall joined Heinz and the Wild Men (sic) about a week ago." As well as Heinz and The Wild Boys, the bill included Marty Wilde and his wife Joyce Baker, and Lulu.

Once Upon A Fairytale was billed as a "pop pantomime" and opened on Boxing Day. Each night there were two performances. The run of dates was scheduled to run through until 23rd January but due to poor ticket sales, after the last night in Norwich the rest of the shows were cancelled.

1964

Date	Venue
Saturday 26th December	Gaumont Theatre, Doncaster, South Yorkshire
Sunday 27th December	Gaumont Theatre, Doncaster, South Yorkshire
Monday 28th December	Gaumont Theatre, Doncaster, South Yorkshire
Tuesday 29th December	Gaumont Theatre, Doncaster, South Yorkshire
Wednesday 30th December	Gaumont Theatre, Doncaster, South Yorkshire
Thursday 31st December	Gaumont Theatre, Doncaster, South Yorkshire

1965

Date	Venue
Friday 1st January	Gaumont Theatre, Doncaster, South Yorkshire
Saturday 2nd January	Gaumont Theatre, Doncaster, South Yorkshire
Monday 4th January	Gaumont Theatre, Norwich, Norfolk
Tuesday 5th January	Gaumont Theatre, Norwich, Norfolk
Wednesday 6th January	Gaumont Theatre, Norwich, Norfolk
Thursday 7th January	Gaumont Theatre, Norwich, Norfolk
Friday 8th January	Gaumont Theatre, Norwich, Norfolk
Saturday 9th January	Gaumont Theatre, Norwich, Norfolk
Wednesday 13th January	Barking, Odeon, East London **CANCELLED**
Thursday 14th January	Barking, Odeon, East London **CANCELLED**
Friday 15th January	Barking, Odeon, East London **CANCELLED**
Saturday 16th January	Barking, Odeon, East London **CANCELLED**
Monday 18th January	Gaumont Theatre, Worcester, Worcestershire **CANCELLED**
Tuesday 19th January	Gaumont Theatre, Worcester, Worcestershire **CANCELLED**
Wednesday 20th January	Gaumont Theatre, Worcester, Worcestershire **CANCELLED**
Thursday 21st January	Gaumont Theatre, Worcester, Worcestershire **CANCELLED**
Friday 22nd January	Gaumont Theatre, Worcester, Worcestershire **CANCELLED**
Saturday 23rd January	Gaumont Theatre, Worcester, Worcestershire **CANCELLED**

Versatile Marty

MARTY WILDE triumphs in his part of Prince William in the "Once Upon A Fairytale" pantomime, which opened at Doncaster Gaumont for the week on Boxing Day.

He handles everything from production numbers to fencing with ease.

Joyce, his wife, a pleasant singer, plays Princess Maria well and Lulu impresses as Witch Hazel. Her diction is first rate. She doesn't have any production songs, but is given three numbers with the Luvvers before the finale.

The family audience showed great appreciation of her rousing "Shout," "Bread-And-Butter" and "Twist And Shout."

Heinz, cast as Captain of the Palace Guard, goes through his hit numbers. But at the opening performance, backing by the Wild Boys was much too loud, and he didn't come over well.

GORDON SAMPSON.

MARTY WILDE

TO take pop stars out of their own little, confined world and put them into pantomime and organised comedy must always be difficult.

Although Marty Wilde has played in many Christmas offerings he will never be at home as a Prince with a magic sword and his single, ten minute session with his guitar must have seemed like heaven to him in "Once Upon A Fairy Tale" (Gaumont Doncaster).

Heinz and his Wild Ones are always lively and when they found their own little niche in their solo spot they were good. But during the rest of the show they gave little indication of being at all at home.

So it was left to little Lulu to provide the bounce and enjoyment and as ever she didn't let anyone down.—F.H.

Pantos close

The two beat pantomimes "Once Upon A Fairy Tale"—starring such artists as Lulu, Millie and Heinz—are being terminated tomorrow (Saturday), and will miss the last two weeks of their scheduled runs because of lack of support.

The Lulu-Marty Wilde-Heinz panto will not now play Barking Odeon (January 11 week) and Worcester Gaumont (18th). The Millie-Jess Conrad show misses Guildford Odeon (11th) and Salisbury Odeon (18th).

January-February 1965 – Neil Christian & The Crusaders

Chris Tidmarsh - lead vocals
Ritchie Blackmore - guitar
Arvid Andersen - bass
Jim Evans - drums

Following the disastrous last couple of months with The Wild Boys Ritchie quickly took some work with Neil Christian (real name Christopher Tidmarsh) and his band. Like The Savages, the band had a reputation of high quality musicians and other notable guitarists such as Albert Lee and Jimmy Page had been in previous line-ups. At these gigs they were billed as Christian's Crusaders.

Only some gigs are listed and I have no idea if the one in Walthamstow was the first but when I was writing *Black Knight* the late Arvid Andersen recalled that with the Crusaders' previous guitarist having quit they were struggling for a replacement when Christian said, "there is one guy left. Ritchie Blackmore, know him?" I had heard of, but never seen the Outlaws. Anyway, Christian came around that afternoon in the band wagon for that night's gig. 'We've got Blackmore, he's doing tonight's show.' We both got into the Bedford Ambulance that Christian had converted and drove to Paul Street in Shoreditch where Chris lived. Someone klaxoned in the street. 'That will be Ritchie, he's in the Ford Consul parked across the way, why don't you go down and say hello' so I did. Ritchie was seated in the front, I tapped on the window, we looked each other straight in the eyes and shook hands. Yes, Ritchie measured up, he looked good, dressed dark, well fitted clothes. We got down to business, no explanation needed; Ritchie ex-Savage rock guitarist not only knew our repertoire but also all the instrumentals. This was a bonus; it was like a kindred spirit. We went on stage without a rehearsal, it was a church hall in the East End." From Andersen's description, this could well refer to the Walthamstow gig.

1965

Date	Venue
Saturday 9th January	Walthamstow Assembly Hall, Walthamstow, London
Thursday 21st January	Royal Star Ballroom, Maidstone, Kent

Supported by The Essex Five.

Friday 19th February	Silver Blades, Streatham, London
Saturday 20th February	Silver Blades, Streatham, London

Arvid Andersen: "When Ritchie joined the Crusaders work was sporadic."

February-May 1965 – Screaming Lord Sutch & The Savages

David Sutch - vocals
Ritchie Blackmore - guitar
Arvid Andersen - bass
Jim Evans - drums
Ashton Tootell - baritone sax
Dick Errington - tenor sax
Noel McManus - tenor sax
Reg Price - tenor sax

It was briefly back to Sutch until some point in mid-May but the exact date it finished is unclear.

1965

Date	Venue
Friday 12th February	Technical College, Farnborough, Hampshire

For this gig they were supported by The Stormsville Shakers. Apparently the saxophonists, referred to as "The Four Saxes" were all dressed in football shirts. According to one of the Stormsville Shakers, as documented on storyofsavages.blogspot.com Ritchie wasn't the guitarist at this gig but another famous name played instead of him. It is possible that he was still with The Crusaders at this stage.

Saturday 13th February   California Ballroom, Dunstable, Bedfordshire
Ritchie definitely played at this gig as documented in Black Knight.

Monday 15th February   Parr Hall, Warrington, Cheshire
Advertised as "The Screaming Lord Sutch Showband." The support act was The Clayton Squares.

Sunday 7th March   Victoria Rooms, Bristol University, Bristol, Gloucestershire
Wednesday 24th March   Top 20 Club, Bradford, West Yorkshire
Monday 29th March   The Hermitage Ballroom, Hitchin, Hertfordshire
Supported by The Cortinas.

Tuesday 27th April   Marquee Club, London
This gig was to promote the launch of the single 'Train Kept A' Rollin".

Sunday 16th May   ABC Alpha Studios, Aston, Birmingham
Recording of 'Train Kept A' Rollin" for Thank Your Lucky Stars. It was broadcasted on Saturday 22nd May.

> SEE **SCREAMIN' LORD SUTCH**
> & THE SAVAGES ON SAT., 22nd MAY
> 'THANK YOUR LUCKY STARS'
> WITH "THE TRAIN KEPT A ROLLING" CBS 201767
> Sole Agents: **KING'S AGENCY** (Variety) LTD.
> 7 DENMARK ST., LONDON, W.C.2 TEM 6303/4

May 1965 – Jerry Lee Lewis

Jerry Lee Lewis - piano, vocals
Ritchie Blackmore - guitar
Arvid Andersen - bass
Jim Evans - drums

The three ex-Savages did a brief stint backing Jerry Lee Lewis at the Star Club in Hamburg. After it Ritchie stayed there, while the other two briefly returned to England.

May 1965-January 1966 – The Three Musketeers

Ritchie Blackmore - guitar
Arvid Andersen - bass
Jim Evans - drums

Arvid Andersen: "Ritchie went on a mission. Flew back to London with the entrepreneur — let's call him AA. He signed us, Jimmy gave up his job — he guaranteed a wage and paid for us to fly to Hamburg. Hamburg was really a workshop. We rehearsed every weekday afternoon in a club. Home to Ritchie meant practice and he really went to work on Les Paul. He bought a two-track recorded and dissected Les Paul, re-recording the guitar tracks in his own style."

"AA had contacts in the clubs. Owned a few himself I believe. As the Three Musketeers we spent about 8-10 months together. We played most Saturday nights in Hamburg and went further afield. Bochum with its Star Club became one of our strongholds. We were sold on to other managers and often did a Hamburg based net worth."

"The original idea was to turn the Musketeers into a four piece with a black guy called Tony Cavanagh. He was a good singer but I did not like the tone. Not rock or even soul. He could hold a melody and was good on stage but not my cup of tea so I showed a general disinterest and he just sort of dropped out."

"The Star Club / Top Ten audiences were great but other venues, especially outside of Hamburg were still honking for James Last."

A fabulous shot of The Three Musketeers with Jimmy Evans double bass drum set up and Ritchie fired up. He always says this is the first band that he really enjoyed.

"I remember the Hamburg days. I first went there in '63 with Jerry Lee Lewis and Gene Vincent but my favourite days were probably in '65 when I was in The Three Musketeers."
15th July 1995

April-September 1966 – Neil Christian & The Crusaders

Chris Tidmarsh - vocals
Ritchie Blackmore - guitar
Tony Dangerfield - bass, vocals
Jim Evans - drums
Tony Marsh - keyboards

Another stint back with Christian.

1966

Date	Venue
Monday 25th April	Town Hall, High Wycombe, Buckinghamshire
Friday 29th April	Wimbledon Palais, Wimbledon, London
Monday 2nd May	Carousel Club, Farnborough, Hampshire
Thursday 7th July	Princess Pavilion, Falmouth, Cornwall
Saturday 9th July	St George's Hall, Exeter, Devon

Support act, The Just Men.

Friday 15th July — Tiles, Oxford Street, London

Support act, The Ray Martin Group.

Saturday 6th August	Town Hall, Tavistock, Devon
Friday 12th August	Lewisham Odeon, London

Opening night of the Swingin' 66 Package Tour in conjunction with Radio England. The tour was headlined by The Small Faces. Some shows of the tour have been listed as having two performances and are marked*. Theoretically in keeping with package tours of the time, all shows had two performances, but in general the tour was poorly attended so some matinee shows could have been cancelled.

Saturday 13th August	Finsbury Park Astoria, London
Monday 15th August	Odeon, Birmingham, Warwickshire
Tuesday 16th August	Gaumont, Sheffield, South Yorkshire*
Wednesday 17th August	Odeon, Leeds, West Yorkshire
Thursday 18th August	Odeon, Glasgow, Lanarkshire
Friday 19th August	Odeon, Newcastle, Northumberland
Saturday 20th August	Odeon, Liverpool, Lancashire*
Monday 22nd August	Odeon, Manchester, Lancashire
Tuesday 23rd August	Capitol, Cardiff, Glamorgan
Wednesday 24th August	Odeon, Exeter, Devon
Thursday 25th August	Odeon, Southampton, Hampshire

Last night of the Swingin' 66 tour.

Thursday 1st September — Winter Gardens, Cleethorpes, Lincolnshire

With support act The Illusions.

Sunday 4th September	Central R&B Club, Central Hotel, Gillingham, Kent
Friday 16th September	Mecca, Grimsby, Lincolnshire

With support act The Fenmen.

October-November 1966 - Riki Maiocchi & The Trip

Riki Maiocchi - vocals
Ritchie Blackmore - guitar
Arvid Andersen - bass
Ian Broad - drums
Billy Gray - rhythm guitar

This gig came via Ian Broad who got the band together with the promise of stacks of work in Italy. They initially went to the Adriatic for a month's residency. When they arrived and took one look at the open-air establishment where they were supposed to be playing they decided to go to Milan where Broad had some connections.

Arvid Andersen: "We were just required to back Riki Maiocchi who had quit a top Italian group (I Camaleonti – The Chameleons) to go solo. He was due out on the road and needed a band. We had a couple of rehearsals and learnt his miserable songs."

1966

Date	Venue
October	The Paip's, Milan, Italy

Several performances are thought to have been done at this club.

| November | Le Roi, Turin, Italy |

This was played early in the month as Ritchie headed back to London to sort out his pending divorce.

| Friday 11th November | 304 Holloway Road, London |

Ritchie records three Glenda Collins tracks for which he was paid a session fee of £9.00. His last session for Meek.

December 1966-April 1967 - Lord Caesar Sutch & The Roman Empire

David Sutch - vocals
Ritchie Blackmore - guitar
Tony Dangerfield - bass, vocals
Carlo Little - drums
Matthew Fisher - organ
Joel James - saxophone

It was back to Sutch once again who had decided to go for a new image and name but to all intents and purposes continued with the same brand of rock 'n' roll.

1966

Date	Venue
December	Fulham, London

Johnny Kidd tribute gig. Band's debut.

| Monday 5th December | Kinema Ballroom, Dunfermline, Fife |
| Sunday 11th December | White Buck, Burley, Hampshire |

With support act Systems Go.

| Thursday 15th December | Sussex University, Brighton, East Sussex |

Supporting Cream.

| Sunday 18th December | Union Rowing Club, Nottingham, Nottinghamshire |
| Saturday 24th December | The Pier Ballroom, Hastings, East Sussex |

With support act Adam Lee Set.

| Saturday 31st December | Blue Lagoon, Newquay, Cornwall |

With support acts The Re-action and The Other Five.

1967

Date	Venue
Sunday 8th January	Britannia Rowing Club, Nottingham, Nottinghamshire
January	Sweden

This was supposedly a ten-day tour with Sutch insisting they wear the Roman style clothing despite the harsh Swedish winter. They were promoting the single 'Purple People Eater' that was only released in Sweden. The gig on the 8th was listed in the Nottingham Evening Post and News on 6th January. Therefore the gig either didn't take place or the Swedish tour wasn't for as long as others have stated. Either way they must have travelled directly from Sweden to Germany.

| Saturday 14th January | Jaguar Club, Scala Herford, Germany |

Supported by The Rainbows. This was the first night of a German tour.

February	Star Club, Kiel, Germany

This was a residency supported by The Xceptions which is thought to have finished on 3rd February, the same day Joe Meek died.

Sunday 12th February	Crown and Cushion, Perry Barr, Birmingham, Warwickshire
Tuesday 7th March	University, Liverpool, Lancashire
Friday 24th March	Kelvin Hall, Glasgow, Lanarkshire
Saturday 25th March	Kelvin Hall, Glasgow, Lanarkshire*
Sunday 26th March	Kelvin Hall, Glasgow, Lanarkshire

These three shows were a multi-band bill including Unit 4+2, Dave Dee, Dozy, Beaky, Mick and Titch, The Mack Sound and The Pirates that included Nick Simper: "As the Pirates relaxed in our dressing room, Dave Sutch came in to ask a favour. He thought it would be a splendid spectacle for the audience to witness a sword fight between him and myself, in Pirate dress. I swiftly pointed out that it made little sense historically to have a Roman Centurion fighting an 18th century pirate, but Dave was so enthusiastic about the idea that I soon found myself agreeing to do it. My cue was to enter stage left, and attack 'Caesar' just as he ignited the tin of petrol-soaked newspaper which was the highlight of his version of the Jerry Lee Lewis classic, 'Great Balls of Fire'. Sutch had provided me with a very piratical sabre which I brandished with gusto, right on cue. Of course, I was not quite prepared for what followed, when Sutch came close to decapitating me with the largest two-handed sword I had ever seen! The audience roared their approval as the fire blazed, whilst Sutch chased me around the stage, accompanied by a blistering Ritchie Blackmore solo. Finally I was forced to leg it for the safety of the dressing room before a demented Sutch could accidentally cause me serious harm!"

*NME advertised a gig for The Uppercut in London on this date so either Sutch only performed the first night, otherwise the London gig never went ahead.

April-May 1967 - Neil Christian & The Crusaders

Chris Tidmarsh - vocals
Ritchie Blackmore - guitar
Tony Dangerfield - bass / vocals
Carlo Little - drums
Matt Smith - piano

They were booked for a one-month tour of Germany, on the back of Christian's big German hit 'Two At A Time'. During this brief spell Ritchie also did his only recording with Christian, the Vogue release 'My Baby's Left Me / Yakity Yak' with Nicky Hopkins on piano, Rick Brown on bass and Carlo Little on drums, although it was not released until the following year.

1967 - Mandrake Root

Ritchie Blackmore - guitar
Ricky Munro - drums
Kurt Lungen - bass
Graham Waller - keyboards

After the tour Ritchie, who had met dancer Bärbel Hardie in April, stayed in Hamburg to put a new band together. He often jammed with other bands in the clubs, while rehearsing his band but no accurate information has been documented. Mandrake Root itself, never got to the point of doing a gig and by December he got a call to go back to the UK where a new band was being formed by some wealthy investors.

Fall of the Roman Empire

Screaming Lord Sutch (above with his Roman Empire) was one of the star attractions of last year's Dances organised by the Social and Arts Committee. This year's bill looks just as good—with Duane Eddy at the Freshers' Ball on Saturday and many other stars to come, including The Kinks, The Tremeloes, The Fourmost, Danta y Pepe, Jimmy Powell and the Dimensions and Mrs. Mary Whitehouse. Mrs. Mary Whitehouse? Yes, the charlady of the National Viewers' and Listeners' Association is giving a Lecture on 23rd October. Sounds interesting.

The Colour Purple: 1968-75

Deep Purple started in a rather lowkey way. Having recorded two songs at Trident Studios in March 1968, a few gigs were set up in Denmark where Jon Lord's previous band The Artwoods had received moderate success. The debut gig was at the Parkskolen (Park School), Tåstrup.

They had decided on the ferry to Esbjerg that they would be called Deep Purple, a name instigated by Ritchie, but as you can see the posters had already been printed up which billed them as Roundabout, the name Chris Curtis had come up with.

This photo is the only one I have ever seen from that first show and gives a wonderful insight into the embryonic days of a band that would in a relatively short time being filling out stadiums and arenas throughout the world.

Deep Purple's first major UK gig was at the annual Sunbury Festival in August. The band did two performances, one on the main stage and one in the marquee.

PROGRAMME

...day 9th August
...IN STAGE
- 8.45 p.m. THE TASTE
- 9.15 p.m. TIME BOX
- 10.00 p.m. JERRY LEE LEW...
- 10.45 p.m. MARMALADE
- 11.30 p.m. THE HERD

...aturday Afternoon...
- 3.00 p.m. MIKE WESTBROOK...
- 3.45 p.m. DON RENDELL - IAN CARR...
- 4.30 p.m. ALAN HAVEN TRIO

...aturday Evening 1...
MAIN STAGE
- 7.00 — 7.30 p.m. DEEP PURPLE
- 7.30 — 8.00 p.m. JOE COCKER
- 8.00 — 8.30 p.m. TYRANNOSAURUS RE...
- 8.30 — 9.00 p.m. TEN YEARS AFTER
- 9.00 — 9.30 p.m. JEFF BECK
- 9.30 — 10.15 p.m. THE NICE
- 9.40 — 10.45 p.m. GINGER BAKER
- 10.15 — 11.25 p.m. ARTHUR BROWN
- 10.45

Sunday Afternoon 11th...
- 2.15 — 3.00 p.m. ECLECTION
- 3.00 — 3.30 p.m. THE JOHNSTONS
- 3.30 — 3.45 p.m. SONYA

Sunday Evening 11th A...
MAIN STAGE
- 7.00 — 7.45 p.m. TRAMLINE
- 7.45 — 8.30 p.m. JOHN MAYALL
- 8.30 — 9.00 p.m. FAIRPORT CONVENTION
- 9.00 — 9.30 p.m. JETHRO TULL
- 9.30 — 10.00 p.m. CHICKEN SHACK
- 10.00 — 10.40 p.m. SPENCER DAVIS
- TRAFFIC

Some of the earliest group publicity photos, with the black and white ones by Tony Gale reported to have been taken at Pictorial Press office, Fleet Street, London on 24th September 1968. September was also the month that the band signed a management deal with HEC Enterprises on the 3rd. As Ian Paice was still under the legal age required his father Keith signed the document on his behalf.

September also saw the release of the debut album *Shades of Deep Purple* in the UK, although it had been released in July in the States, where the initial success occurred.

In both countries it was predated by the single release 'Hush'. Initially both countries also released special promotional versions of the single but it was only America that bought the record in sufficient quantities, which saw it reach number 4 on the Billboard chart. In the UK, 'Hush' was initially released on Friday 21st June but was largely ignored. EMI reissued it on 27th September but it was always thought, at least by the band, that EMI was more preoccupied with The Beatles.

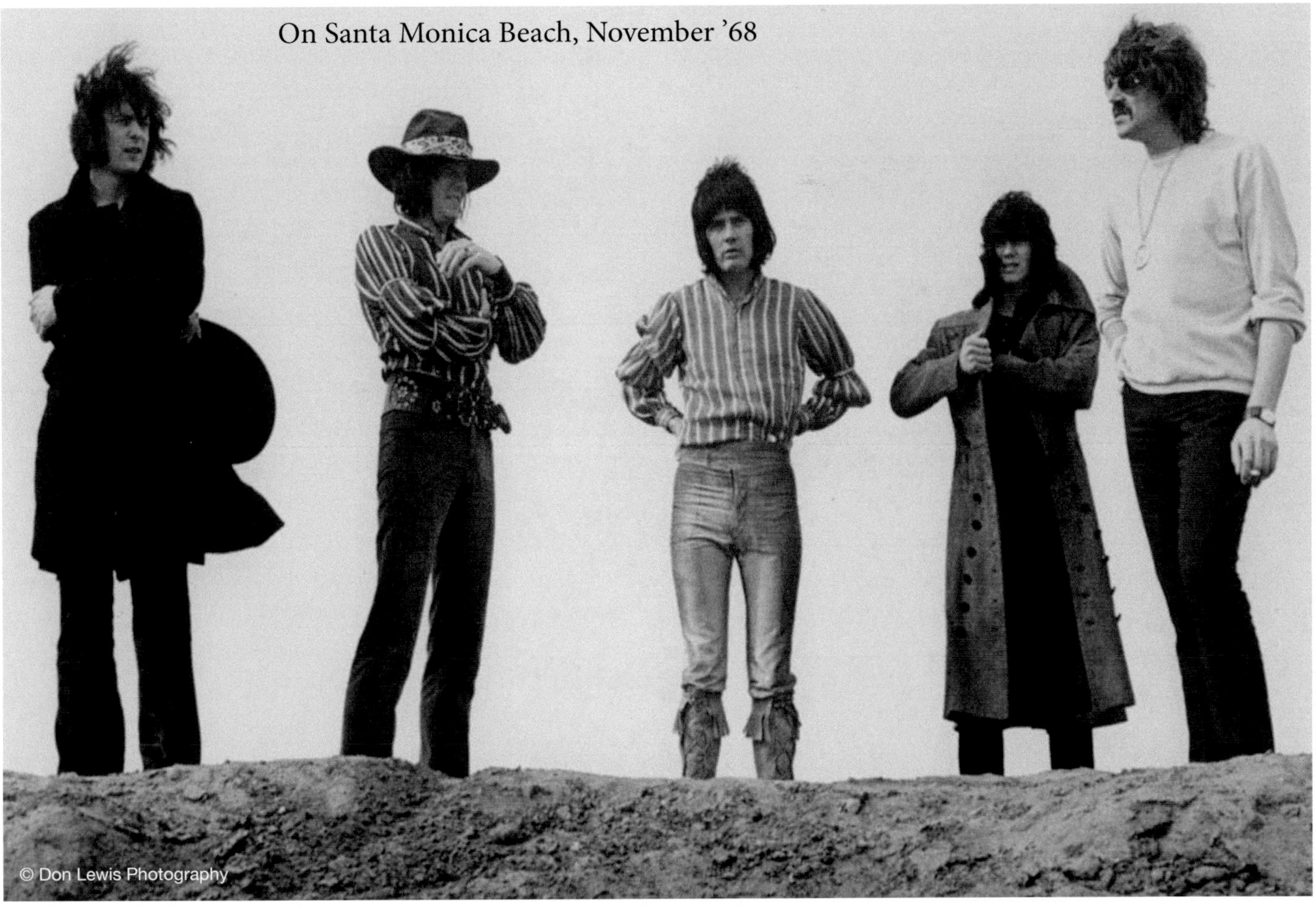

On Santa Monica Beach, November '68

© Don Lewis Photography

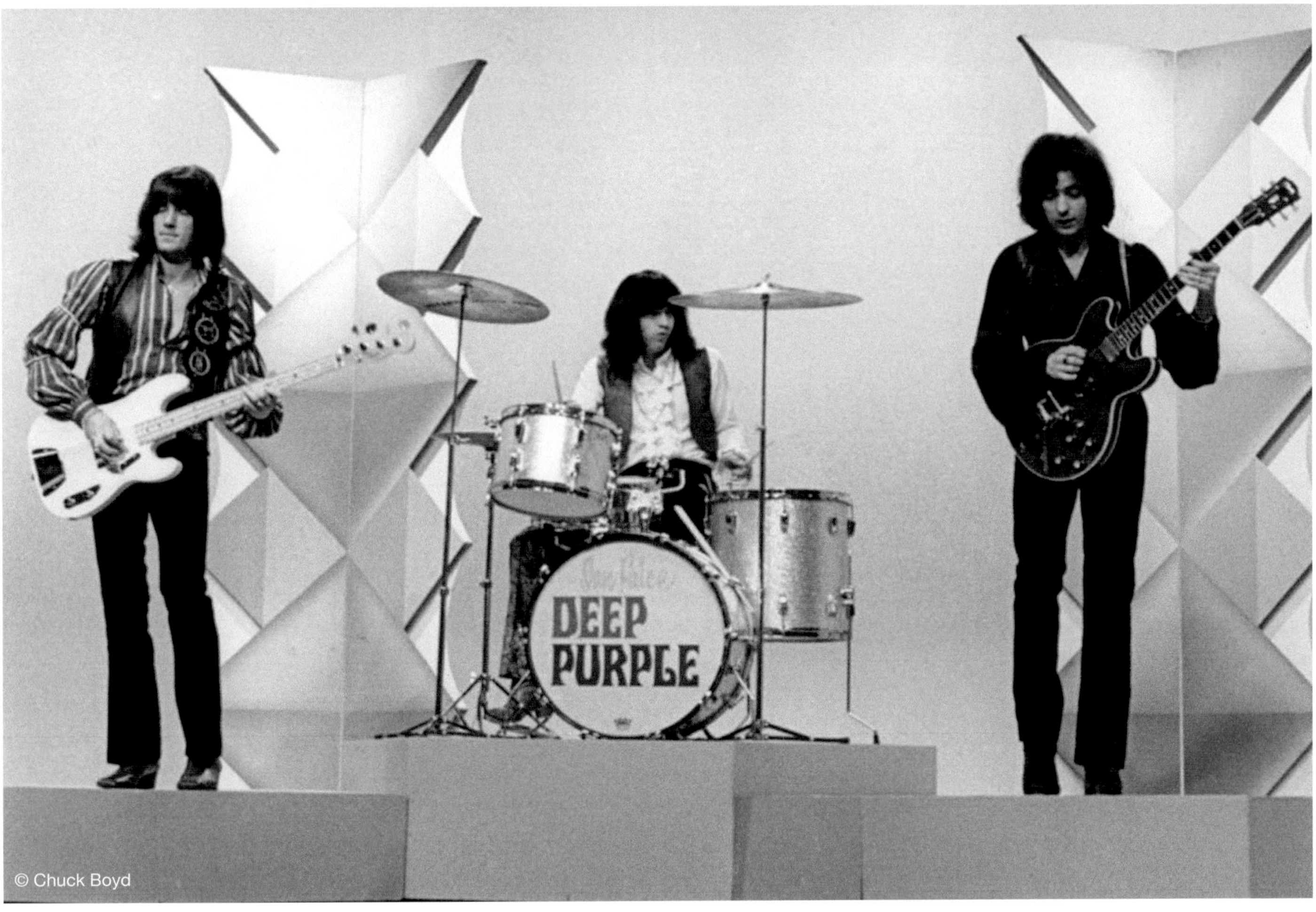

© Chuck Boyd

Thanks to the initial success of 'Hush', as well as the promotional weight of Tetragrammaton Records, Purple did several TV appearances during the first year of the band's existence. Sadly the original footage for many of these performances appear to no longer exist.

By the summer of '69 the second incarnation of Deep Purple had played their first few gigs with a major event at the Royal Albert Hall looming. However, before that there was the small matter of tying the knot for the second time at Acton Registry Office, on 16th September.

The wedding to Bärbel Hardie was a lowkey event with Deep Purple roadie Mick Angus (far left) and Ritchie's brother Paul (far right) being the signatory witnesses. At the back between Angus and Ritchie is Deep Purple producer Derek Lawrence although his time in that capacity with the band had already come to an end.
(Courtesy of Babs Blackmore)

Although Ritchie is on record as voicing his lack of enthusiasm for Jon Lord's Concerto For Group & Orchestra, there is no doubting his performance on the night was magical. This shot is from the rehearsals earlier in the day.

At De Lane Lea, Studios in London during the making of the promotional film for 'Black Night'. De Lane Lea was integral to Deep Purple's early recordings. Situated on London's Kingsway, De Lane Lea had been the studio used for the recording of the second and third albums. Both 'Speed King' and 'Hard Lovin' Man' from *In Rock* were also recorded there, as well as some of the *Fireball* album.

"I was nearly put inside for a couple of months once. The Outlaws had policemen waiting around when we did sessions because they knew we would cause trouble. We were a bit mad. We'd play at places and really smash them up. We got a lot of bills and not many return bookings."
Melody Maker, 1970

© Araldo Di Crollalanza/Globe Photos/ZUMAPRESS.com

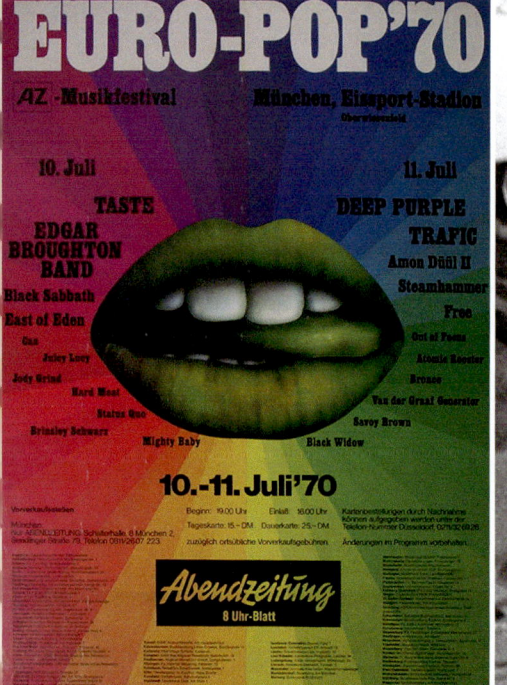

"Our new one is certainly the nearest to what we are like on stage. And it's the first to represent the band as it is now. It's much harder, raucous and exciting. That is what we are trying to get across, rather than musical ability. It's hard and simple. I hate the last three LPs. I think bands should be exciting live. There are so many groups going round with a hidden message — and they are so boring. I didn't really enjoy the thing we did with the orchestra. But I was happy for Jon. We don't write together now like we used to, but we're not growing apart musically. We both like each other's stuff. He's happy now he's done his concerto and happy just to play with the band."
Disc & Music Echo, June 1970

© Philippe Gras / Alamy Stock Photo

Two contrasting shots from La Taverne de L'Olympia in Paris on 8th October 1970 that was filmed for the *Pop Deux* TV show broadcasted on French TV. It showcased the dynamism of Purple's set at the time, which still relied heavily on older material such as 'Wring That Neck' and 'Mandrake Root'. Those numbers perfectly embodied Ritchie's improvisational abilities, with each piece invariably being stretched out to half an hour each. No such chance for a half hour TV show, although the performances were edited down to fit the schedule.

© Philippe Gras / Alamy Stock Photo

Palazzo dello Sport, Rome, 25th May 1971. Purple played two shows in one day; an afternoon show and an evening one.

This next selection of photos all come courtesy of Babs and are of Ritchie at his then home in Camberley in 1972. He had his own pub built into part of the house that he named Blockhütte — the name of the bar in Hamburg where he met Babs in April 1967. The photo of the pair of them together is with their beloved dog Stroichie.

"There are times I think someone else is playing for me. Once at the Star Club, Hamburg, I felt two hands coming round from behind me as if someone else was playing, someone who was very good. I've never had that sensation since, but I've never forgotten it."
Disc & Music Echo, May 1972

Long Beach Arena, California, 15th April 1973. By now Purple was one of the biggest bands in the world and capable of filling arenas across America, from west to east and north to south but the friction between Blackmore and Gillan had ripped the band apart. Gillan had already informed the band he was leaving but despite the personal clashes, on stage the band was still as cohesive and the performances were just as exciting and powerful as they had been in 1969.

© Jeffrey Mayer, Pictorial Press Ltd / Alamy Stock Photo

Deep Purple $$-Breaker

LONDON—Deep Purple have become the world's highest paid group after concluding a deal claimed to be worth $500,000 to play one televised concert in America.

The announcement, by Purple's co-manager John Coletts, came shortly after the Osmonds established themselves as top-money group after finalizing a contract with a Las Vegas Theatre.

The pop idols will receive $5 million to appear six times a week for eight weeks a year over the next four years. This works out at about $26,000 per appearance. Deep Purple's record shattering concert, in California on April 6, will be televised on Don Kirshner's "In Concert" program.

The show is wedged in between what was to be a two-week break between the conclusion of a tour of America and a 24-concert tour of the U.K. starting mid-April.

FEBRUARY 2, 1974, **BILLBOARD**

A change of line-up with David Coverdale and Glenn Hughes replacing Gillan and Glover didn't diminish the band's popularity. Indeed the catalogue of work by MkII had elevated Purple beyond their wildest dreams.

The height of success culminated with the band's appearance at the California Jam on 6th April 1974. A mammoth one-day concert at the Ontario Motor Speedway. The exact crowd figure will never be accurately ascertained but estimates put it at somewhere between 250,000 and 400,000.

Ritchie made the most of the event with his explosive finale to 'Space Truckin'' as documented in the ABC TV footage of the event. The photos here include shots taken from different angles to the TV broadcast.

© Jeffrey Mayer Pictorial Press Ltd / Alamy Stock Photo

59

After the huge tour of the States the Burn tour moved on to the UK. Deep Purple's homeland didn't have an array of large arenas at the time and the tour comprised of smaller venues such as Birmingham Town Hall on 4th May 1974.

"The hardest thing in this business is sincerity. Once you can fake that you're laughing!"
King's Hall, Belle Vue, Manchester, 15th May 1974

© Laurens van Houten / Frank White Photo Agency

(© Laurens van Houten / Frank White Photo Agency)

(© Laurens van Houten / Frank White Photo Agency)

(© Laurens van Houten / Frank White Photo Agency)

Despite sometimes playing it down, Ritchie was heavily influenced by Jimi Hendrix in much of his stage presence. Left handed Hendrix would often been seen playing right-handed guitars, and as can be seen here, the right-handed Blackmore is playing a left-handed Strat. All part of the showmanship that he had crafted over several years.

"On stage? Never. I get nervous off stage. Life frightens me more than music. I like my solitude, that's why I don't socialise as much as people want me to. I keep to my own dressing room. I like to tune my guitars up - I've so many to get in tune. I like to sit back and relax, have a drink and go and watch the other band. I go and sit in the audience. I always have to do that then I can get a vibe of what they want just by looking at them."

Guitar (USA), August 1974

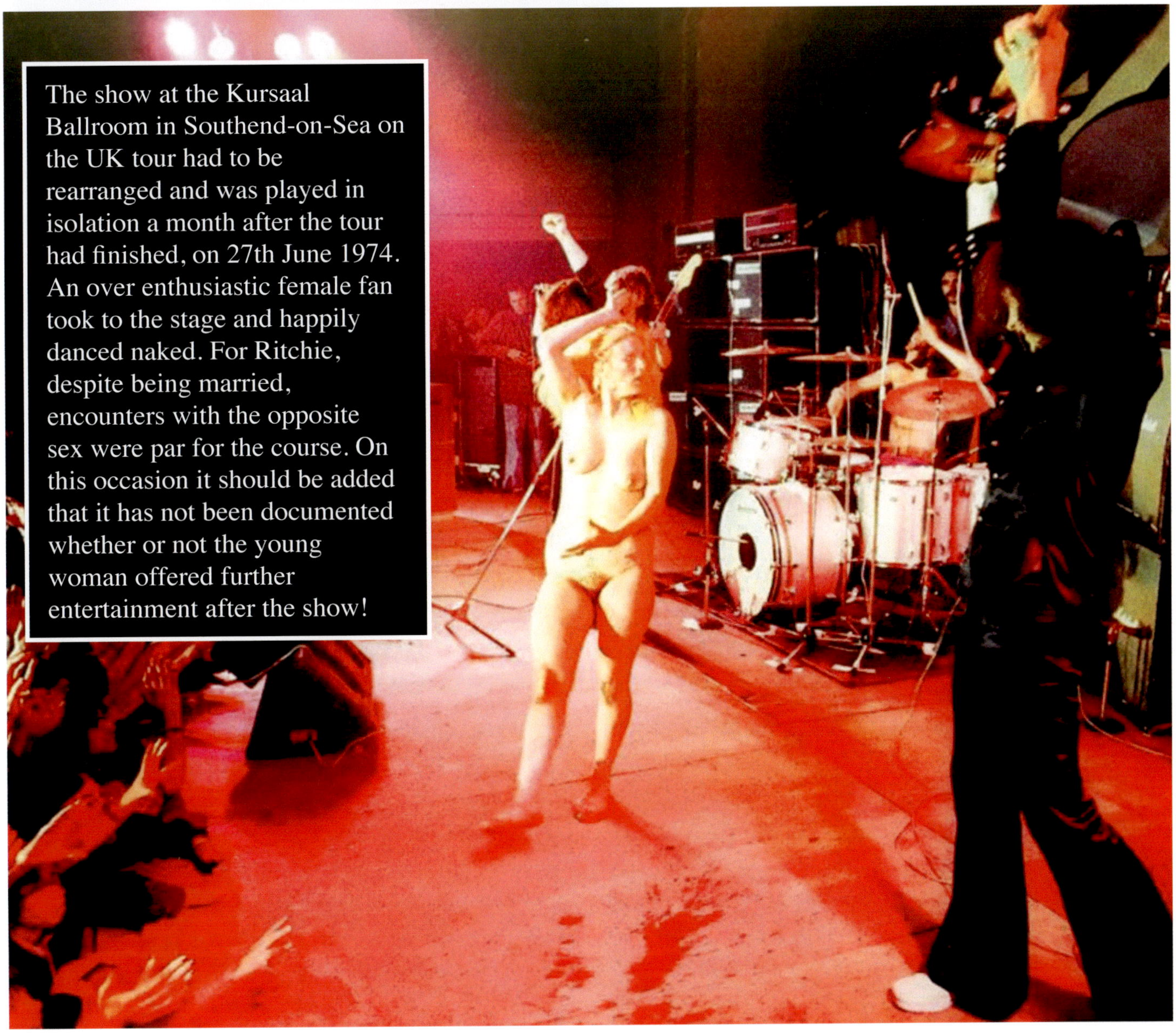

The show at the Kursaal Ballroom in Southend-on-Sea on the UK tour had to be rearranged and was played in isolation a month after the tour had finished, on 27th June 1974. An over enthusiastic female fan took to the stage and happily danced naked. For Ritchie, despite being married, encounters with the opposite sex were par for the course. On this occasion it should be added that it has not been documented whether or not the young woman offered further entertainment after the show!

Deep Purple returned to America for a few huge stadium shows in the summer of '74, followed by a German tour in September.

Stadthalle, Bremen,
18th September 1974

It was back to the States again from mid-November through to mid-December. During the tour Ritchie laid down two tracks for a planned solo single, his first for a decade. Helped by the support band Elf, it set the seed for his next move. As such the US tour was to be his last with Deep Purple in the seventies.

Long Beach Arena,
Los Angeles,
20th November 1974.

© Jeffrey Mayer Pictorial Press Ltd / Alamy Stock Photo

Ritchie's final gigs with Deep Purple were in Europe in March and April 1975.

Backstage after the last show in Paris with Ian Broad, Colin Hart and at the front Purple Music manager Graham Nolder.

With Colin Hart, who went with Ritchie as Rainbow's tour manager from day one.

A New Spectrum: 1975-84

Although the first Rainbow album was recorded before Ritchie's last European tour with Deep Purple, the release didn't happen until several months later by which time Blackmore had already reshuffled the pack and was putting together a band ready to go out on the road.

This sequence of photos were all taken at Rainbow's first US show at the Beacon Theatre, New York, 12th November 1975.

© Frank White

Community Theatre, Berkeley, California, 28th November 1975

Rainbow's pivotal album Rising was recorded at Musicland Studios in Munich in February 1976. A very convivial time, with the album recorded in a matter of a few days. Ritchie and Jimmy Bain captured in playful mood by tour manager Colin Hart.

"I like Stargazer very much because we had great fun having the orchestra dubbed on. The original concept was made on the cello. I'd played the cello for two years and the only thing I could play was that riff and a few others. But it was a different way of doing a rock song. It was quite interesting seeing all the cellists playing something that I'd played within two months."
Australia, 21st November 1976.

Rainbow on the rise

RAINBOW have completed recording their new album which has been tentatively set for release at the end of April — but they won't be seen in Britain before August when they plan to do a tour.

Titled 'RAINBOW Rising', the album was recorded in 10 days at Munich's Musicland Studio but the tapes are being taken to America for mixing. All compositions are from within the group — Ritchie Blackmore, Ronnie James Dio, Tony Carey, Jimmy Bain and Cozy Powell.

Blackmore told SOUNDS: "I can't take the music to pieces but if I'm forced into a description I'd say it's a kind of long, heavy rock with a lot of melodic content that seems to be missing from a lot of today's rock and roll groups."

A single from the band, likely to be 'Tarot Woman', will be issued in mid-April shortly before the album and before the band start their American tour.

BLACKMORE

"Jon Lord loved it (Rainbow Rising) when he heard it."
Circus, 1st June 1976

Martin Birch with his back to the camera, with Ritchie and Ronnie during the making of Rising.

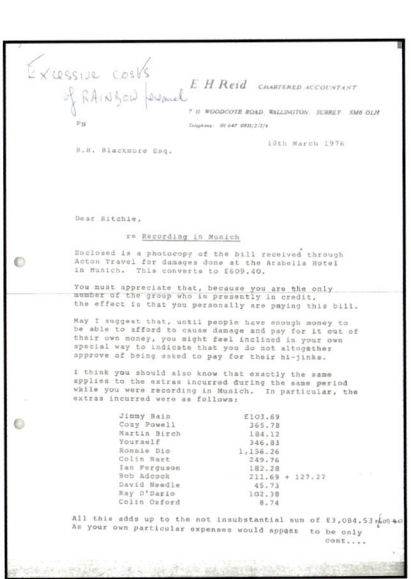

BLACKMORE'S RAINBOW

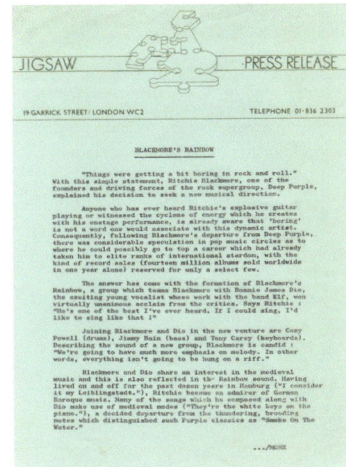

The penultimate show of the US leg of the Rising tour was at Civic Auditorium, San Jose, California, 6th August 1976, where these photos were taken. It was only the US leg where both 'Stargazer' and 'A Light In The Black' were played. The latter was dropped thereafter although it was played at a couple of Japanese dates as well.

© John Oyster

© John Oyster

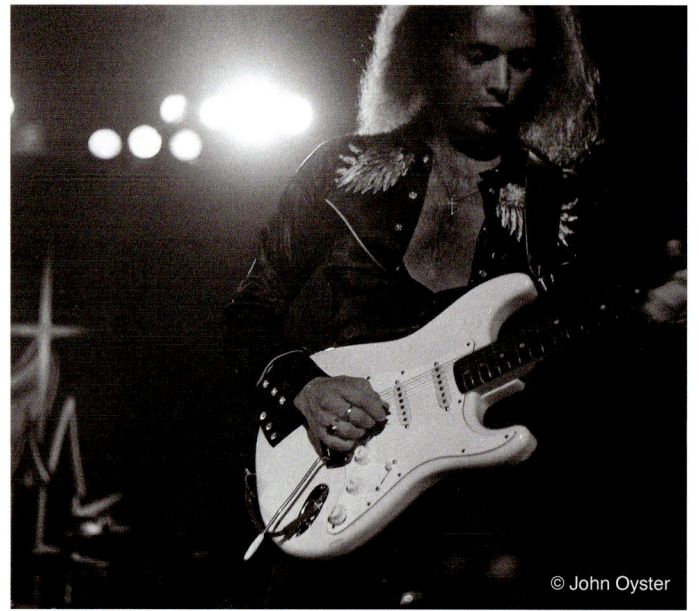

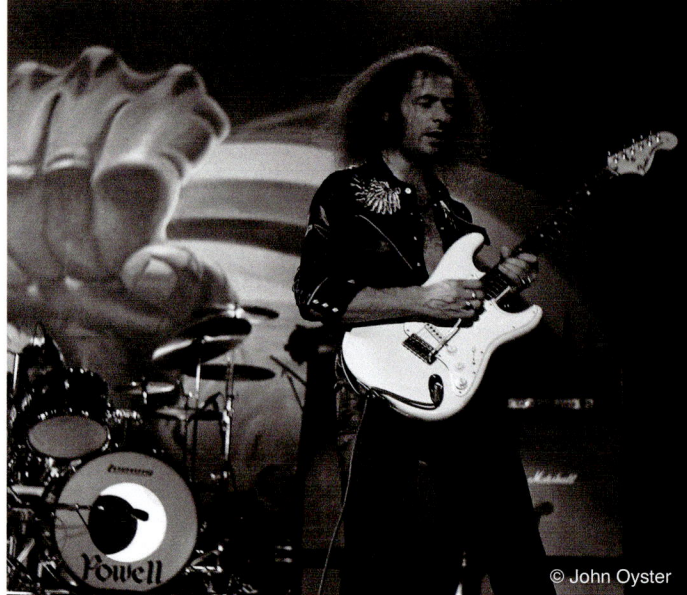

Musikhalle Grosser Saal, Hamburg, 23rd September 1976.

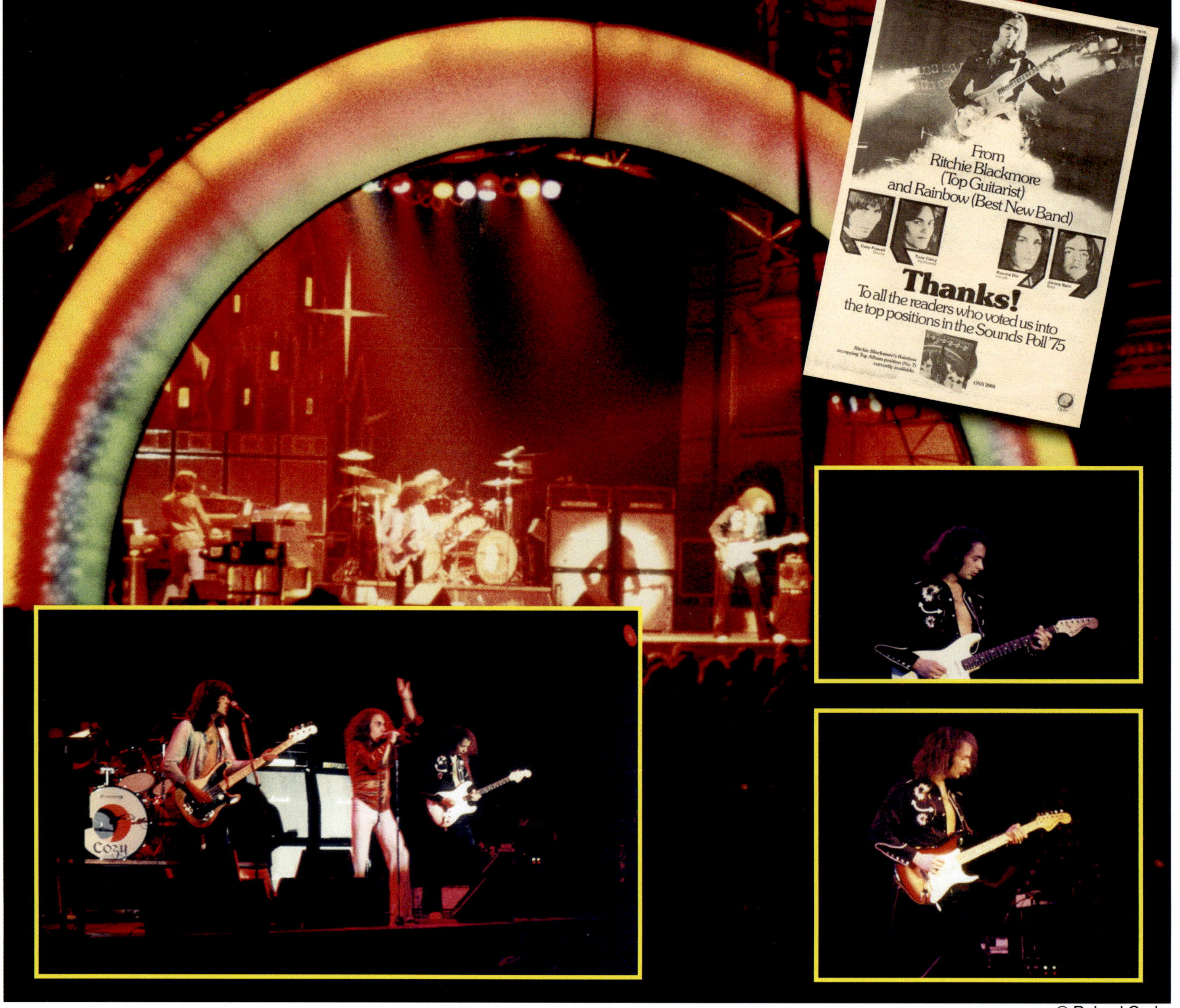

© Roland Guder

At a party at Ronnie James Dio's in 1977 with his then girlfriend Susan Davis.

Backstage at the Congresgebouw, The Hague, Netherlands, 4th October 1977

Enjoying some time out in England during the 1977 UK tour.

Empire Theatre, Liverpool, 5th November, 1977. For non-UK fans, the 5th of November is known as Guy Fawkes Night, or Bonfire Night, where fireworks are a customary part of the tradition. Whether or not Ritchie was thinking about that during the gig is unclear, but he certainly created fireworks of his own towards the end of the show. He climbed into the royal box and started demolishing his guitar, causing significant damage to the building, and prompting the management to ban him from the venue.

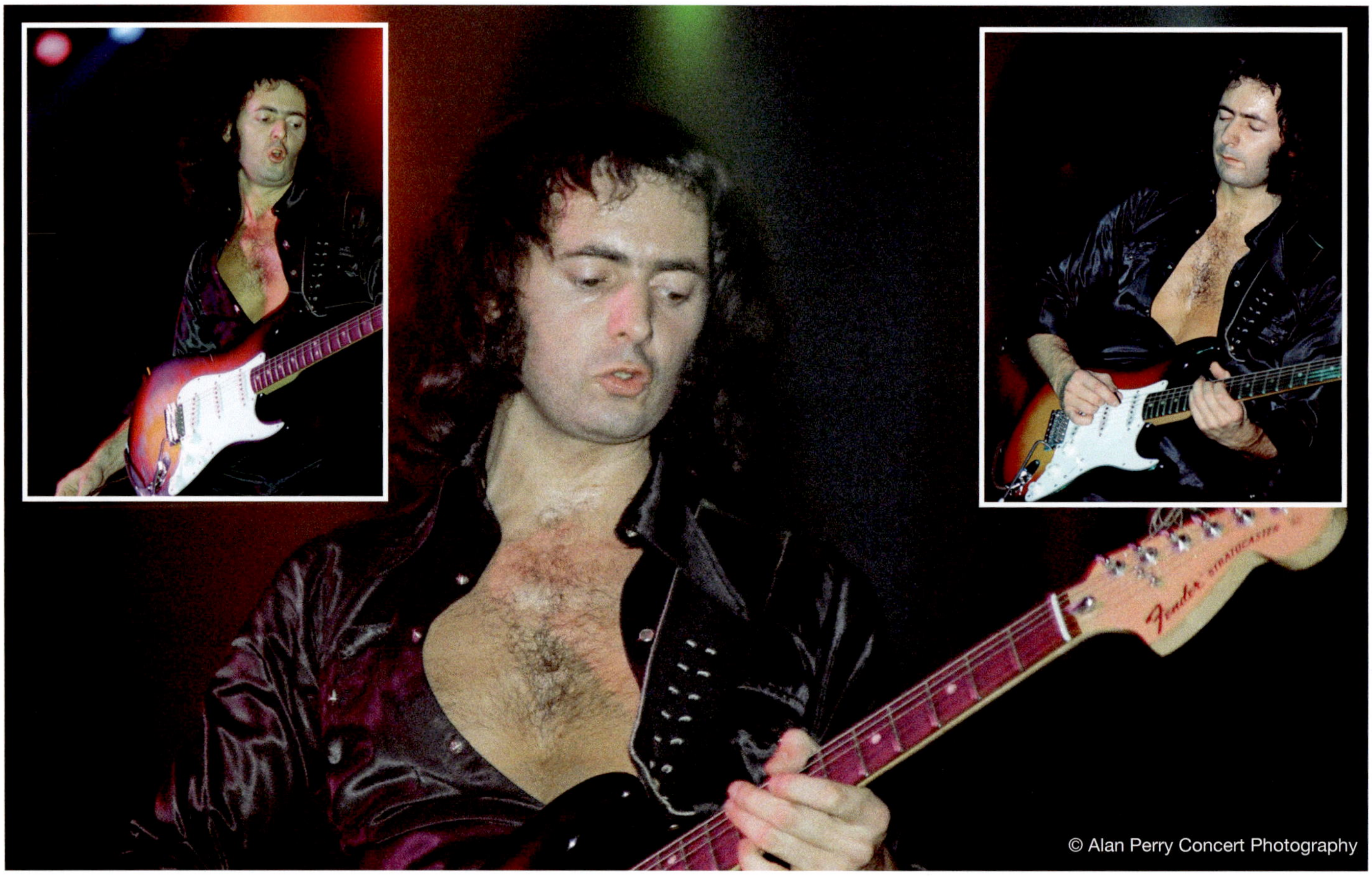

© Alan Perry Concert Photography

Festival Hall, Melbourne, Australia, November 1976

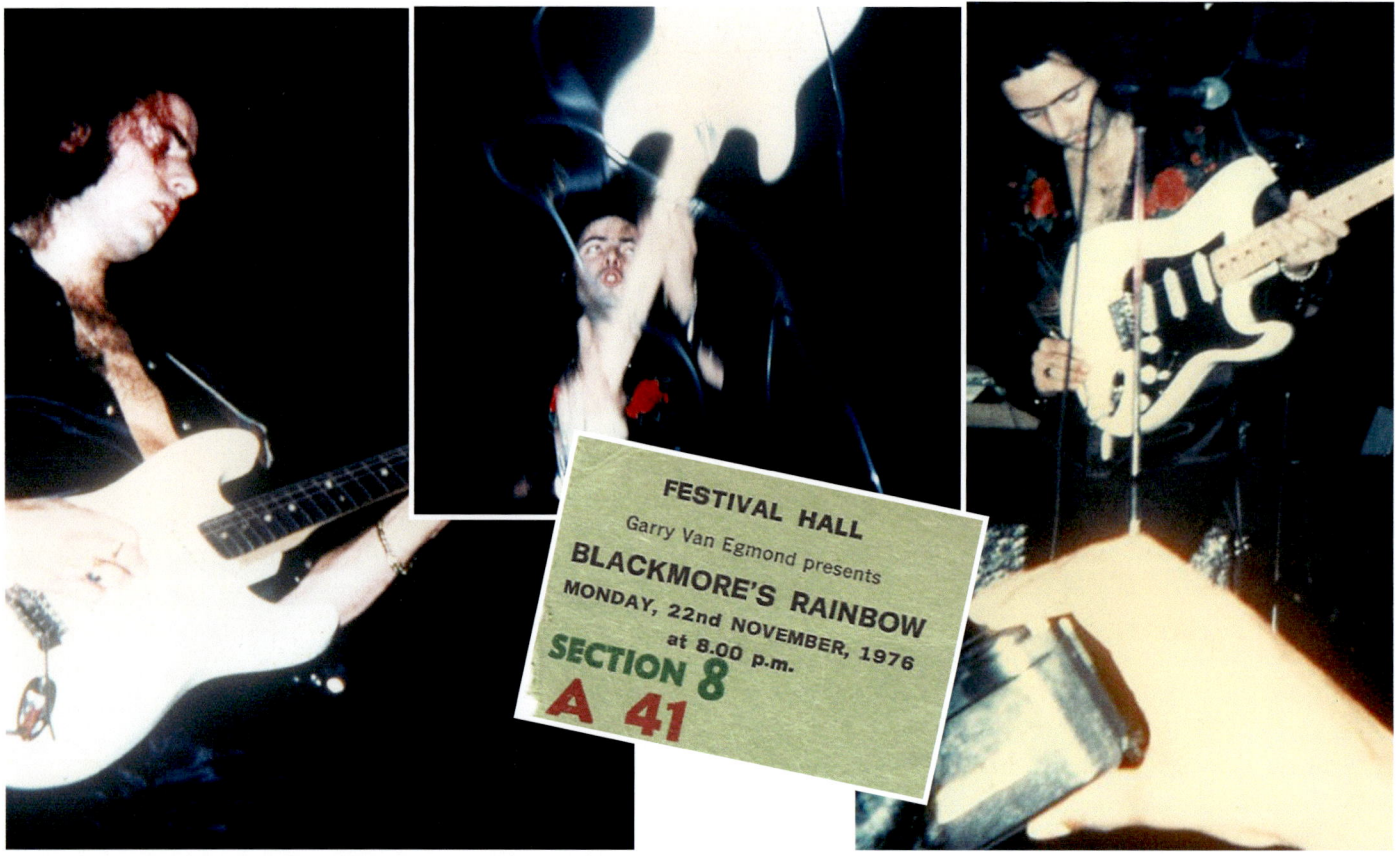

With Bob Daisley at Ronnie's wedding in Connecticut, 7th April 1978.

A concerted effort to increase Rainbow's popularity in the States occurred through the summer of '78. An extensive tour that ran from the 9th May through to 24th August. It was to be the last tour with Ronnie James Dio.

© Ed Rottinger / Thompson Music Management

By December '78 Ronnie James Dio had parted with the band and Ritchie's initial thought was to replace him with Ian Gillan. The pair met up to discuss it, but despite jamming with Gillan's band at the Marquee on 27th December, nothing came of it.

Ritchie's then girlfriend Amy Rothman, sandwiched between him and Ian Gillan.

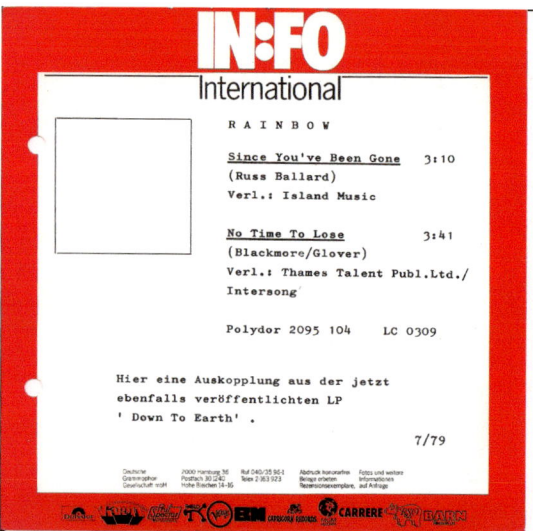

By 1979 the revamped Rainbow with Roger Glover, Don Airey and Graham Bonnet launched the Down To Earth album and toured the world promoting it. Once again the initial port of call was the States where they toured extensively from September through to December. Initially as a support act to Blue Oyster Cult and then headlining.

© Lynn McAfee (Lebrecht Music & Arts / Alamy Stock Photo

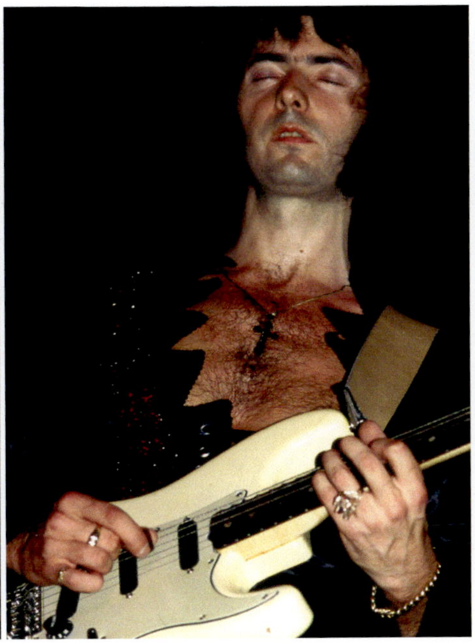

© Lynn McAfee (Lebrecht Music & Arts / Alamy Stock Photo)

Touring in Europe commenced in January 1980 and the UK leg kicked off with two shows in Newcastle on 19th and 20th February. The following sequence of shots come from the second night.

© Alan Perry Concert Photography

© Alan Perry Concert Photography

A tour of Japan followed the UK. Here Ritchie can be seen travelling on the bullet train.

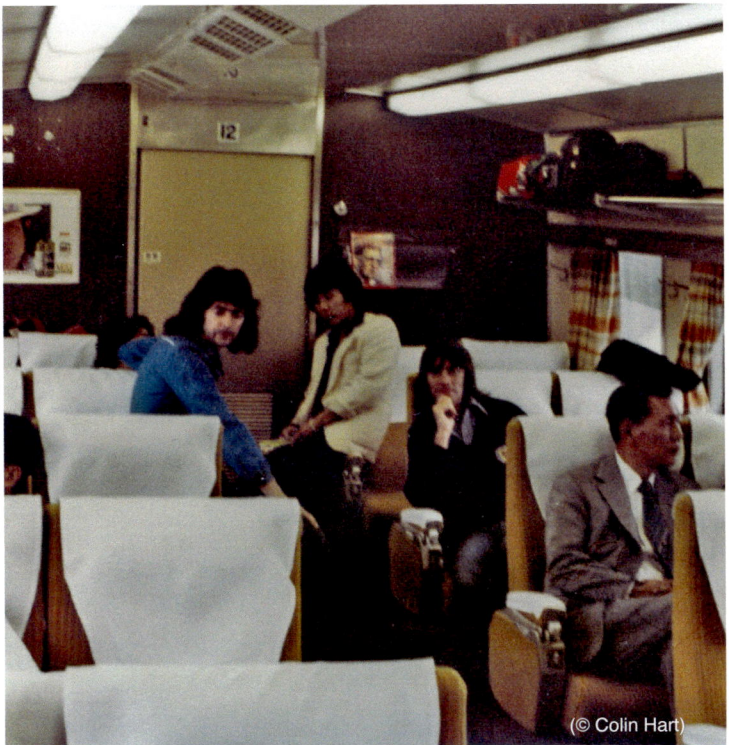

(© Colin Hart)

IN:FO

International

RAINBOW

ALL NIGHT LONG 3:49

(Blackmore/Glover)

Thames Talent Publ. Ltd.

WEISSHEIM 5:10

(Blackmore)

Panache Music Ltd.

Polydor 2095 196 LC 0309

Leider liegt die neue Rainbow-Single erst zum Schluß der Europa-Tournee vor. Grund dafür sind die völlig neu aufgenommene Rückseite "Weissheim" (Ritchie Blackmore nennt so sein Haus in Los Angeles als Erinnerung an seine Zeit in Deutschland) und eine neue Abmischung des A-Titels.
Sowohl live wie auf der Platte zeigt sich, wie entscheidend und optimal eingepaßt Graham Bonnets Gesang die geänderte Besetzung und den Stil der Gruppe beeinflußt.

2/80

Deutsche Grammophon Gesellschaft mbH · 2000 Hamburg 36, Postfach 30 1240, Hohe Bleichen 14–16 · Ruf 040/35 96 1, Telex 2-163 923 · Abdruck honorarfrei, Belege erbeten, Rezensionsexemplare, Fotos und weitere Informationen auf Anfrage

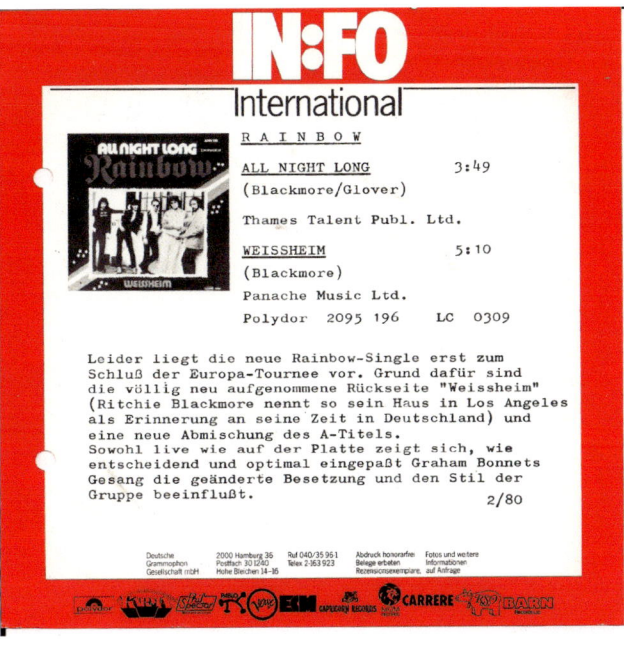

This short-lived incarnation of Rainbow concluded in the summer of ’78 with their biggest show, headlining the first Monsters OF Rock Festival at Donington Park on 16th August. Cozy Powell had decided to move on to pastures new after five years with Ritchie, and although he didn’t know it at the time it was to be Graham Bonnet’s last show as well.

Once again, Ritchie ensured there would be an explosive finale, which was also captured on film and shown on UK TV on 9th October during BBC’s week of rock performances billed as Rock Week Concert. The half edit was eventually released on disc in April 2016.

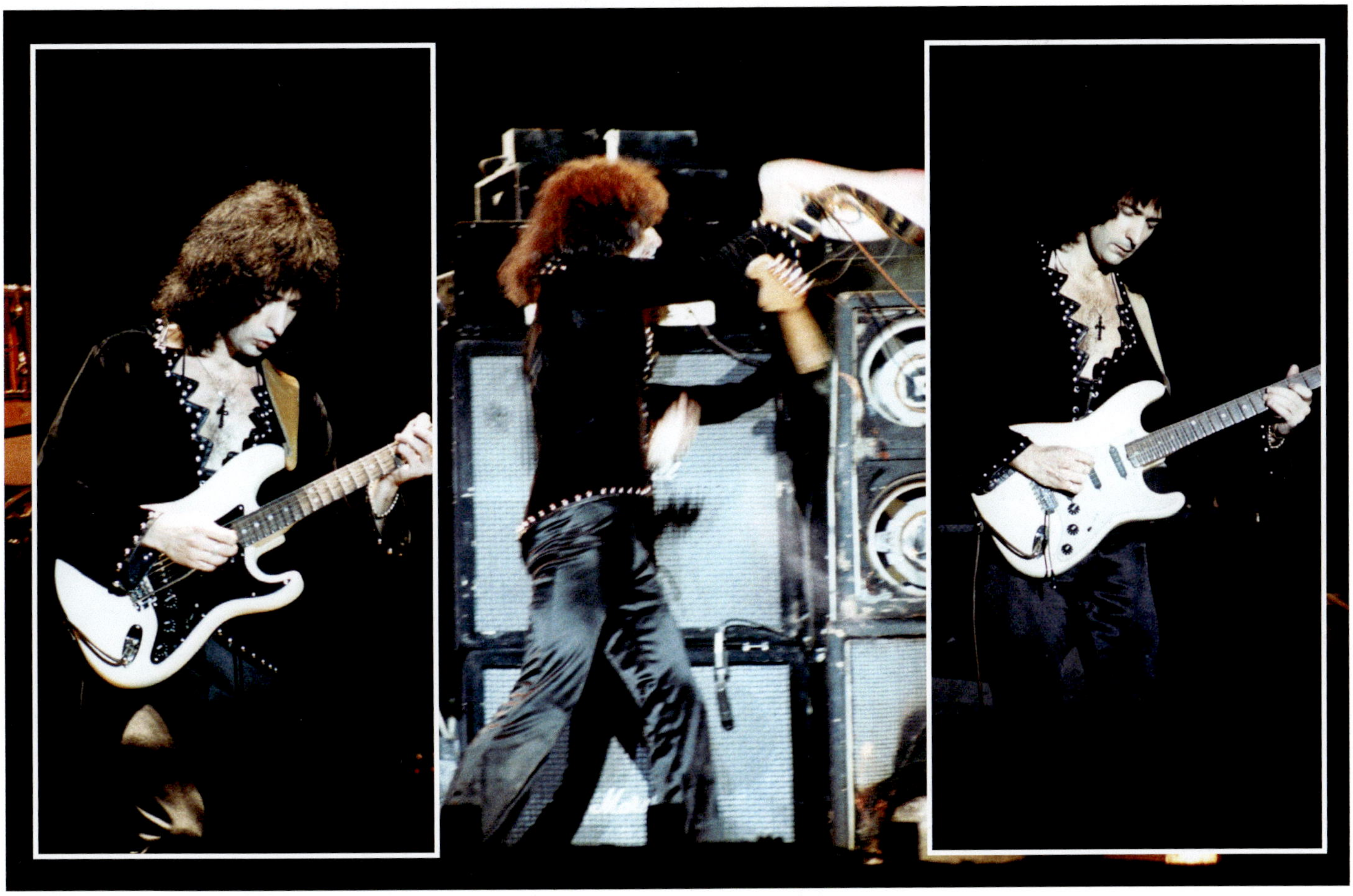

By late 1980, now with Joe Lynn Turner on vocals, Rainbow secured its status and started to get the degree of recognition that Ritchie was so keen to have in the States.

With the release of *Difficult To Cure* in early 1981, the single from the album, 'I Surrender' gave Rainbow its biggest UK hit, peaking at number 3, but once again touring commenced in the States between February and May.

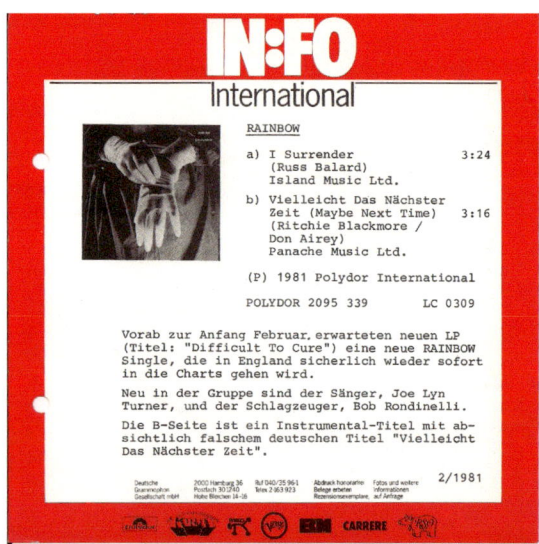

Capitol Theatre, Passaic, New Jersey, 8th May 1981

As soon as the tour was finished, Ritchie tied the knot for the third time when he married Amy Rothman on 16th May. Manager Bruce Payne's wedding present was this moped that the bride and groom are seen with.

Recording *Straight Between The Eyes* at Le Studio in Quebec, Canada, December 1981

Although Rainbow's popularity in the States never attained the same level as Deep Purple, by 1982 the band had built up to the point that it could now play at the prestigious 20,000 capacity Madison Square Garden in New York. It was the pinnacle of Rainbow's career in the biggest rock market in the world.

Madison Square Garden, New York, 19th June 1982

© Frank White

© Frank White

© Marc Brans

More Purple Passages: 1984-1993

Despite Rainbow having attained more commercial success over the years, the lure of a Deep Purple reunion was too lucrative to ignore and in early 1984 the classic MkII line-up reunited.

Initially it was as if they had never been away. The *Perfect Strangers* album was a strong return with all the typical Deep Purple hallmarks with a 1980s feel and reflecting the influences and styles that they had all attained in the intervening years.

During the mixing of the album in Hamburg, Germany in September 1984 the band played in front of a live audience for the first time since 29th June 1973 when they got up and jammed at Night Club One, although because there were no keyboards Jon Lord had to be content with playing "air organ" on the bar!

Ritchie with his girlfriend of the time Tammi Williams.

A mammoth world tour that started in late '84 and ran through to the summer of '85 was one of the rock highlights of the time. The US leg was the second biggest grossing tour that year. Deep Purple was back in force.

© Mick Gregory

© Mick Gregory

The set lists were pretty much based around *Perfect Strangers* and *Made In Japan* but Ritchie also included his adaptation of Beethoven's 'Ode To Joy' from the Ninth Symphony which he had rebranded as 'Difficult To Cure' on the album of the same name.

© Mick Gregory

Teaming up with the old adversary Ian Gillan was initially a joyous occasion and this was reflected in the performances during the tour.

Deep Purple's solitary concert on home soil was effectively on home mud as the Knebworth Festival turned out to be one of the wettest June days of all time. Ritchie played the show in his Wellington boots.

Two days later the gig was guaranteed rain free at the indoor Limburghall, Genk, Belgium on 24th June.

At some performances Ritchie would swap instruments with Roger during the ending to 'Smoke On The Water'.

Deep Purple played two nights in Paris. Both were filmed by WDR TV, with the second night's showed broadcasted. During the performance of 'Black Night' Ritchie led Gillan and Glover into the Shadows dance routine.

Sporthalle, Cologne,
8th February 1987

© Marc Brans

Despite Ritchie's image as the man in black for much of the 1987 and '88 tour dates he alternated between a purple suede jacket and a green leather one. He has often stated that green is his favourite colour.

"My fantasy is to form a medieval band playing Renaissance music. I have a good 16th century repertoire; all I've got to do is find the other players."
Kerrang!, 1987

Vorst National, Brussels, 21st February 1987.

Despite the friction that started to develop after the first album and tour, there were still moments on stage when Ritchie and Ian Gillan were having a whale of a time such as at this show at the Olympiahalle in Munich, 17th February 1987.

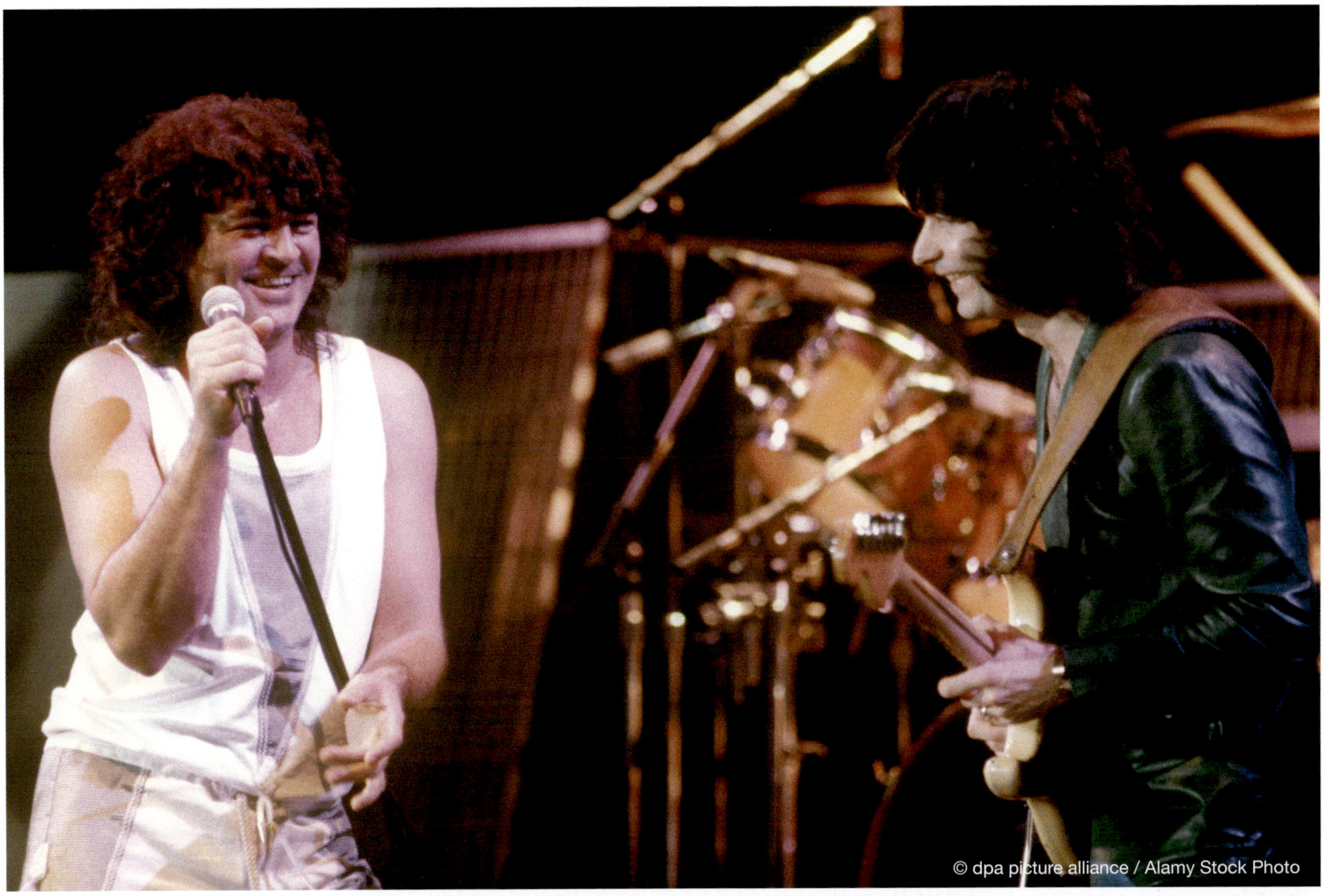

© dpa picture alliance / Alamy Stock Photo

Purple headlined at Giants Stadium, East Rutherford, New Jersey on 16th August 1988. They were supported by Aerosmith and Guns N' Roses. Although no one could foresee it at the time, it turned out to be the last gig that the classic MkII line-up would play on American soil.

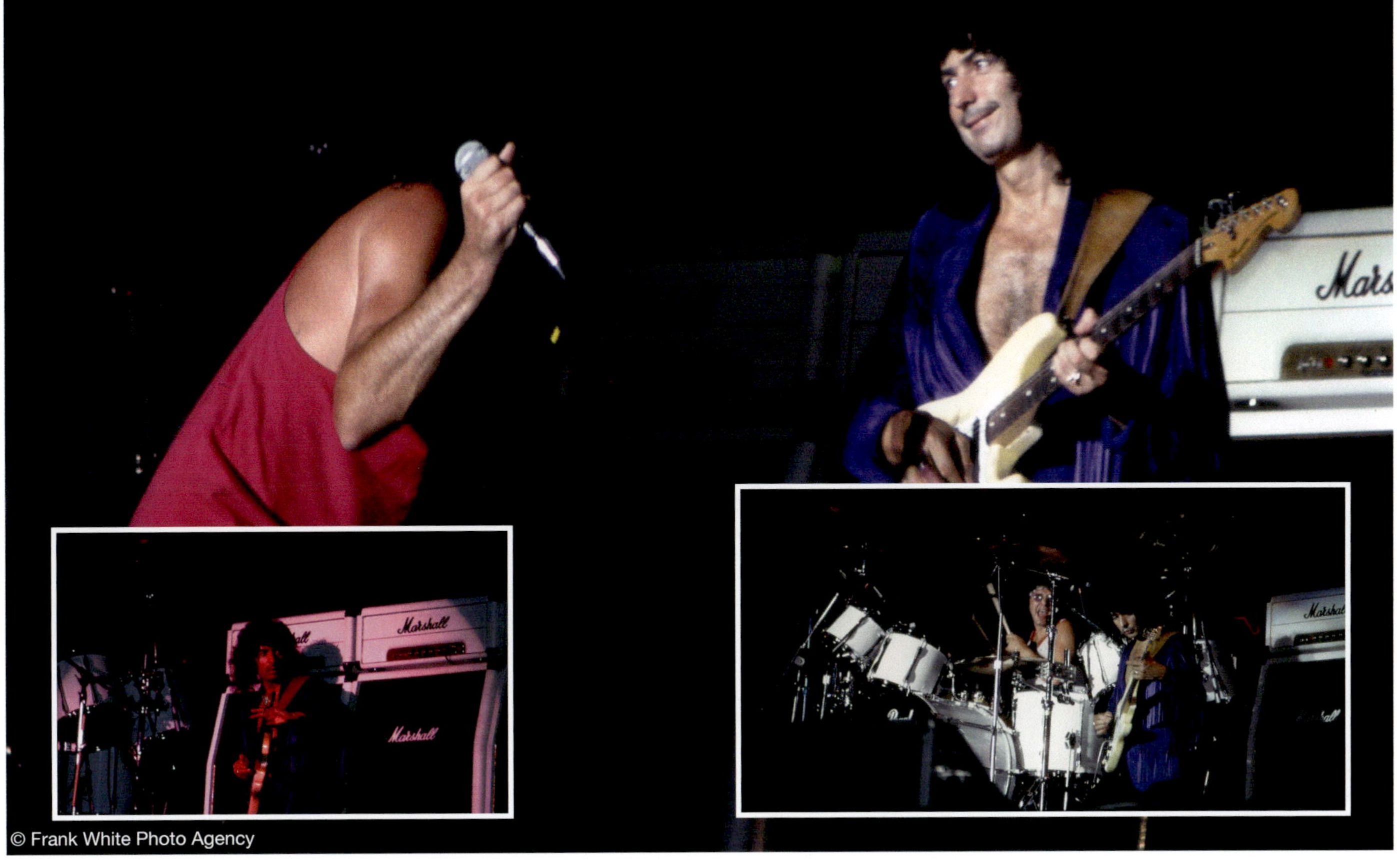

© Frank White Photo Agency

A short European tour in September '88 would prove to be the last dates of MkII for five years, as Ritchie ousted Ian Gillan from the band the following year. Despite trying several replacements, by the time Deep Purple recorded the next album former Rainbow vocalist Joe Lynn Turner had been brought in.

Rehearsing for what would become the Slaves & Masters album in Vermont early 1990.

This line-up of Deep Purple only played a handful of shows in the States. Many gigs were cancelled due to poor ticket sales. Partly a knock on effect from having cancelled shows in '87 when Ritchie broke his finger on stage; partly due to the general change in the US music scene; partly due to the line-up change and partly due to American audiences fickle nature and loss of interest in Deep Purple since they had lapped the band up in 1985.

Ritchie however was more than happy with the way things were going and this reflected in his playing throughout the tour. When Deep Purple had reformed in 1984, there was a feeling, and something he later admitted, that he felt the need to change and compete with the new kids on the block — guitarists such as Eddie Van Halen, Steve Vai and many others who had gained a reputation since Deep Purple's halcyon days in the seventies. By the nineties his playing appeared to have loosened.

© Frank White

To make up for the loss of sales in the American market, the '91 tour saw the band play several new territories such as Thailand, Singapore and Israel. They also did several shows in Brazil. Here is Ritchie in transit at an airport in Brazil on 24th August, the day of the last Brazillian show in Rio de Janeiro.

Also as the tour progressed Ritchie was sending postcards from around the world to a young American lady, Candice Isralow who he had met in Long Island when Deep Purple had played a football match against the radio station that she worked for.

An avid, keen footballer, Ritchie has always taken opportunities to fit in games on tour. Doing so in a country so fixated on football as Brazil was simply inevitable and Ritchie also splashed out on a new kit for the game.

Relaxing with Joe on 10th December 1991.

As progress was slowly being made on the follow-up to *Slaves & Masters,* for one of the rare times in his life, Ritchie found himself overruled by the rest of the band as he was given the ultimatum of getting Ian Gillan back in the band.

By November '92 Gillan re-joined Deep Purple as they finished off the album in Germany. Few words were exchanged between he and Ritchie.

A world tour was announced, planned to start in the States but as in '91 ticket demand was poor and the tour was cancelled. Fortunately the same wasn't the case for Europe and 37 dates were played from late September through to November. Although the friction with Ian Gillan was palpable the performances were amongst the best from the reformed Deep Purple.

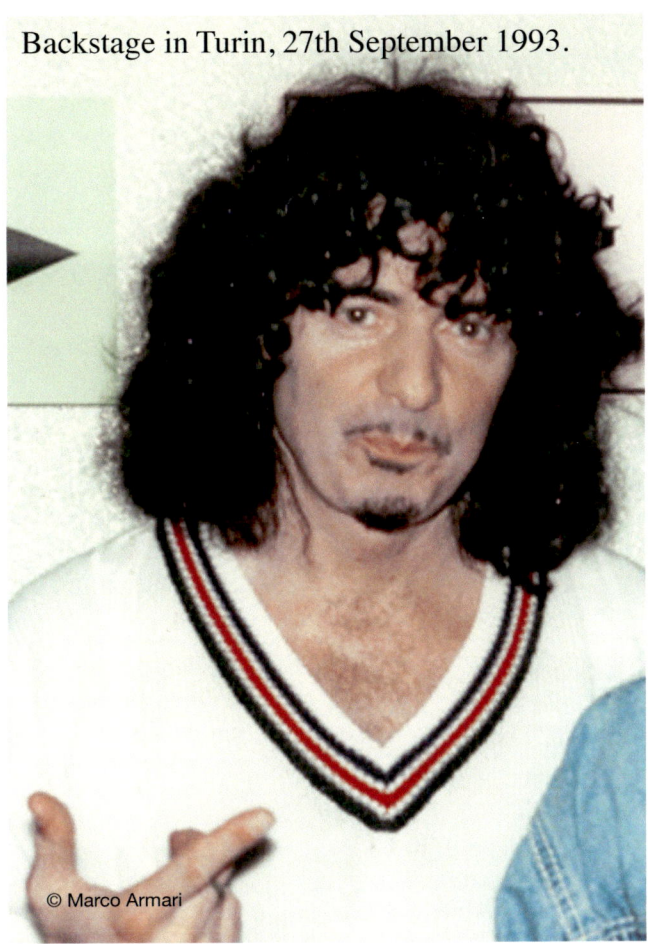

Backstage in Turin, 27th September 1993.

Ritchie was accompanied on the tour by his new girlfriend Candice.

Patinoire de Malley, Lausanne, 22nd October 1993

Backstage in Germany during the tour. For twenty years Ritchie had shown an interest in mediaeval and renaissance music, so the lute should come as no surprise.

A happy looking Ritchie, relaxing with Candice during the '93 tour. By the time of the show in Prague he even got Candice to supply backing vocals from the side of the stage for Beethoven's Ninth.

Afternoon football at Hurlingham Park in Fulham before the second Brixton show, 8th November 1993.

Backstage at the NEC before the show. Ritchie had strained his ankle the night before at Brixton when he slipped at the start of the show and was advised by a doctor not to play. He ignored the advice but certainly caused a lot of drama as documented in the film of the Birmingham gig.

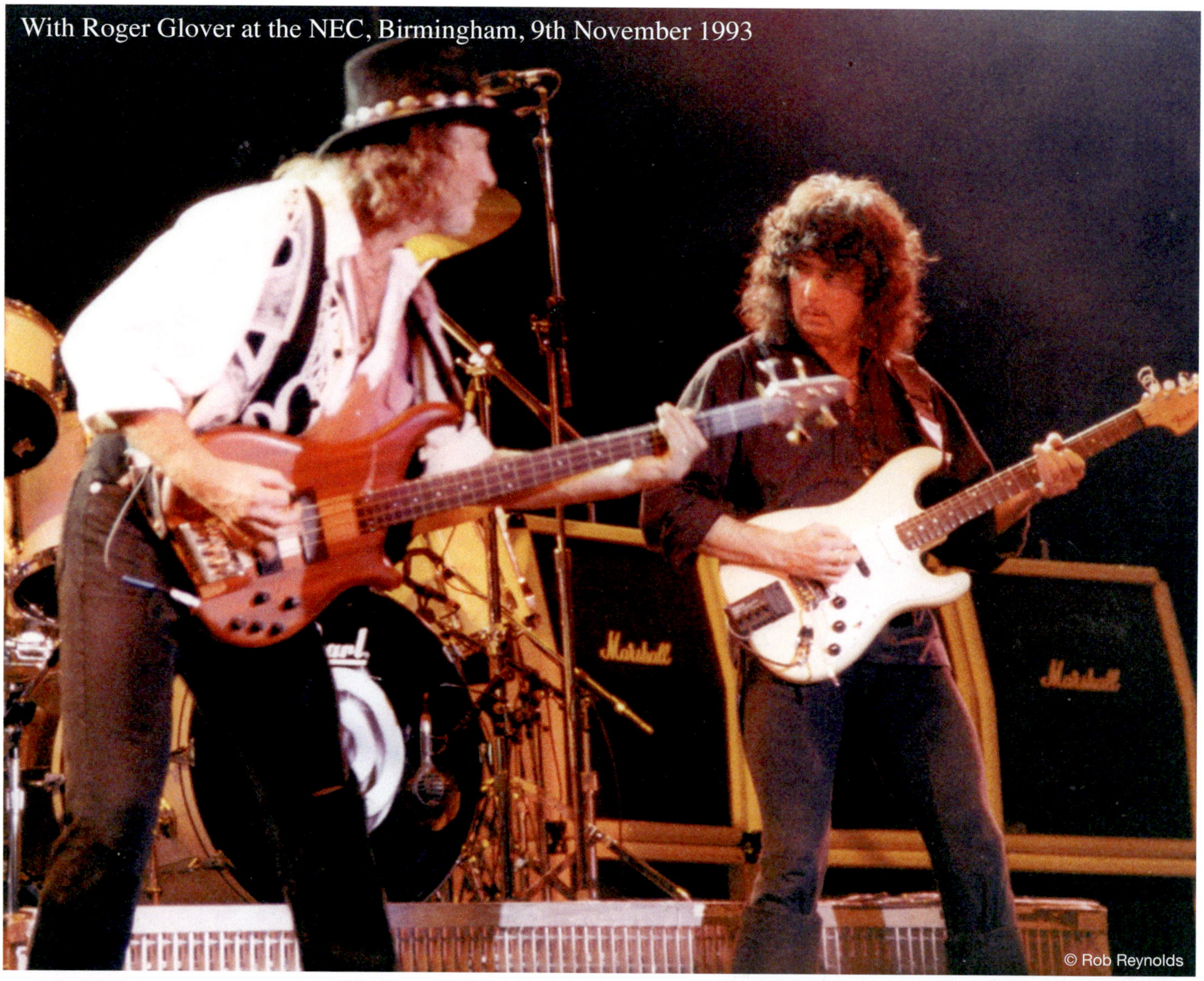

With Roger Glover at the NEC, Birmingham, 9th November 1993

© Rob Reynolds

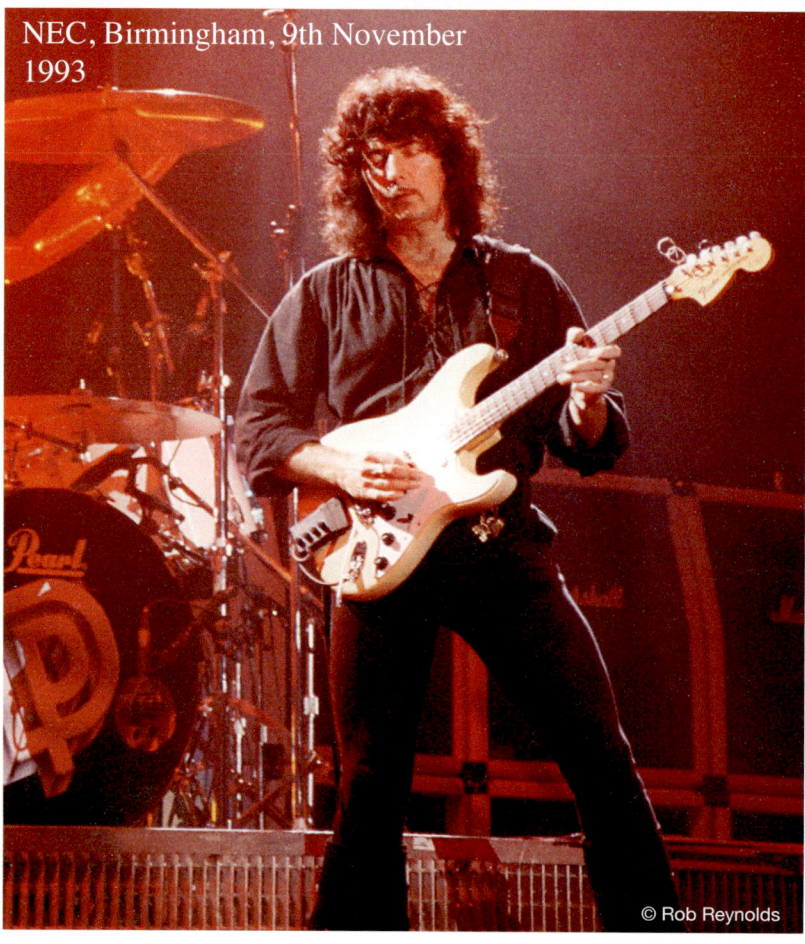

NEC, Birmingham, 9th November 1993

© Rob Reynolds

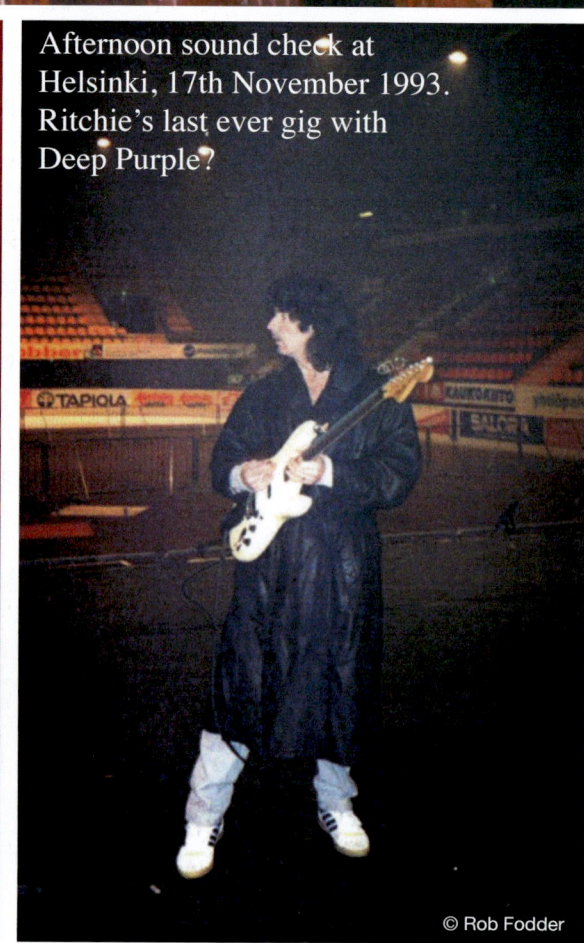

Afternoon sound check at Helsinki, 17th November 1993. Ritchie's last ever gig with Deep Purple?

© Rob Fodder

Reflecting The Rainbow: 1994-1997

There's no doubt that Ritchie's departure from Purple for the second time in 1993 was a lot more acrimonious than when he quit in 1975. He soon took stock of his situation however and started to put a new band together. Initially he wanted to start completely afresh although his idea for the band name of Rainbow Moon was clearly designed to acknowledge his past. By the time plans had become more formulated, record company pressure ensured that he simple reverted to Rainbow.

"It wasn't an act of reformation but it is a new group. I wanted to differentiate this group from Rainbow by christening it Rainbow Moon, the principal reason being that I feel a strange attraction to this heavenly body. In addition it was the name of my grandmother, for whom I have a great admiration. I finally changed my mind noting that a whole bunch of groups were calling themselves Moon this or Moon that.
I am happy with Rainbow. At least the people will know what they are dealing with."
Hard & Heavy, France, 1995

With a new band of relatively unfamiliar faces, they got to know each other as they performed casually in the local bars in Long Island and later Massachusetts, once they started to work on the album *Stranger In Us All*.

Having supplied backing vocals on a couple of the Purple shows, Ritchie also encouraged Candice to be involved with the album and she contributed lyrics to some tracks. Doogie White was the chief songwriting collaborator who also had a full knowledge of Ritchie's back catalogue.

In some wonderful kind of symmetry, The new look Rainbow's first show was on 30th September 1995 in Helsinki — the same city that Ritchie had done his last show with Purple almost two years earlier.

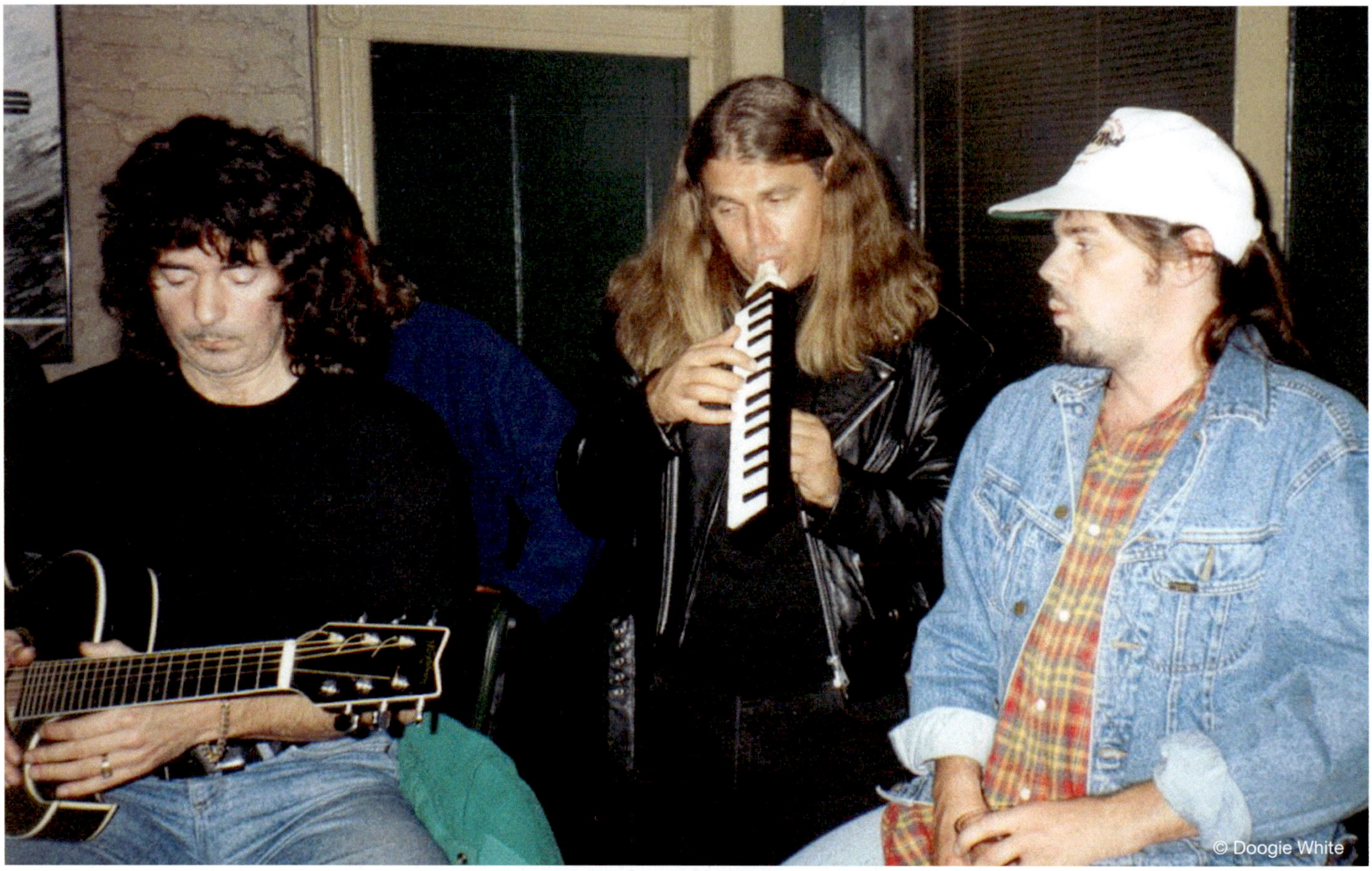

© Doogie White

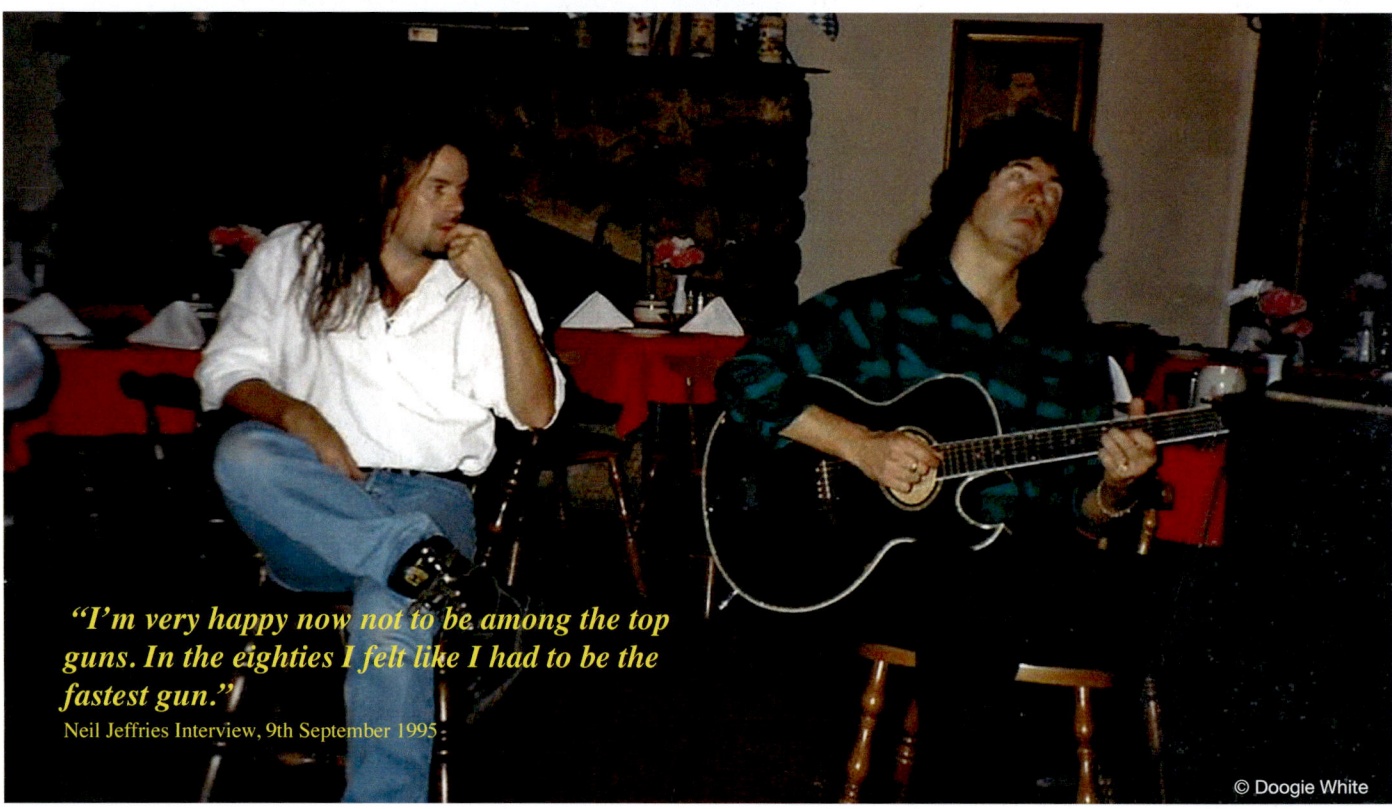

"I'm very happy now not to be among the top guns. In the eighties I felt like I had to be the fastest gun."
Neil Jeffries Interview, 9th September 1995

© Doogie White

Gemeentehal, Vosselaar, Belgium, 28th July 1996

An impromptu performance at the Balingen Festival on 21st July, just after Rainbow had finished their set on the main stage. Ritchie and Doogie White did an acoustic set in the marquee.

In Passau, Germany, 26th July, 1996 with Horst Langer from Engl, with the very first Ritchie Blackmore Engl 150 signature amp and a certificate indicating it, signed by both of them.

Performing at the Serenadenhof, Nuremburg, Germany, 30th July 1996

"The older I get the more fun I want. I don't play anymore to impress musicians."
Guitar & Bass, Germany, 1995

Backstage in Nuremburg.

With the author backstage in Nuremburg.

Bad Wörishofen, Germany, 3rd August 1996

20th February 1997 was the opening night of the nineties Rainbow's one and only US tour at the Birch Hill Nite Club, Old Bridge New Jersey where these photos were taken.

*"I'm actually too insecure to play with other guitarists;
I'm frightened that someone will wipe the floor with me."*
Guitar & Bass, Germany, 1995

A European tour was planned to follow it, but several dates were cancelled including Poland. It left just the one show, as Rainbow headlined on the 31st May at the Esbjerg Rock Festival in Denmark.

Also on the bill was Peter Green's Splinter Group that featured Cozy Powell. Ritchie and Cozy spent several hours together reminiscing and later on even discussed the possibility of a reunion along with Ronnie Dio.

As it was, the show in Esbjerg was the last Rainbow show… many thought for ever, as Ritchie focused on his new project of Blackmore's Night from that point on. Straight after the show Ritchie and Candice headed to Germany for a promotional trip for *Shadow Of The Moon*.

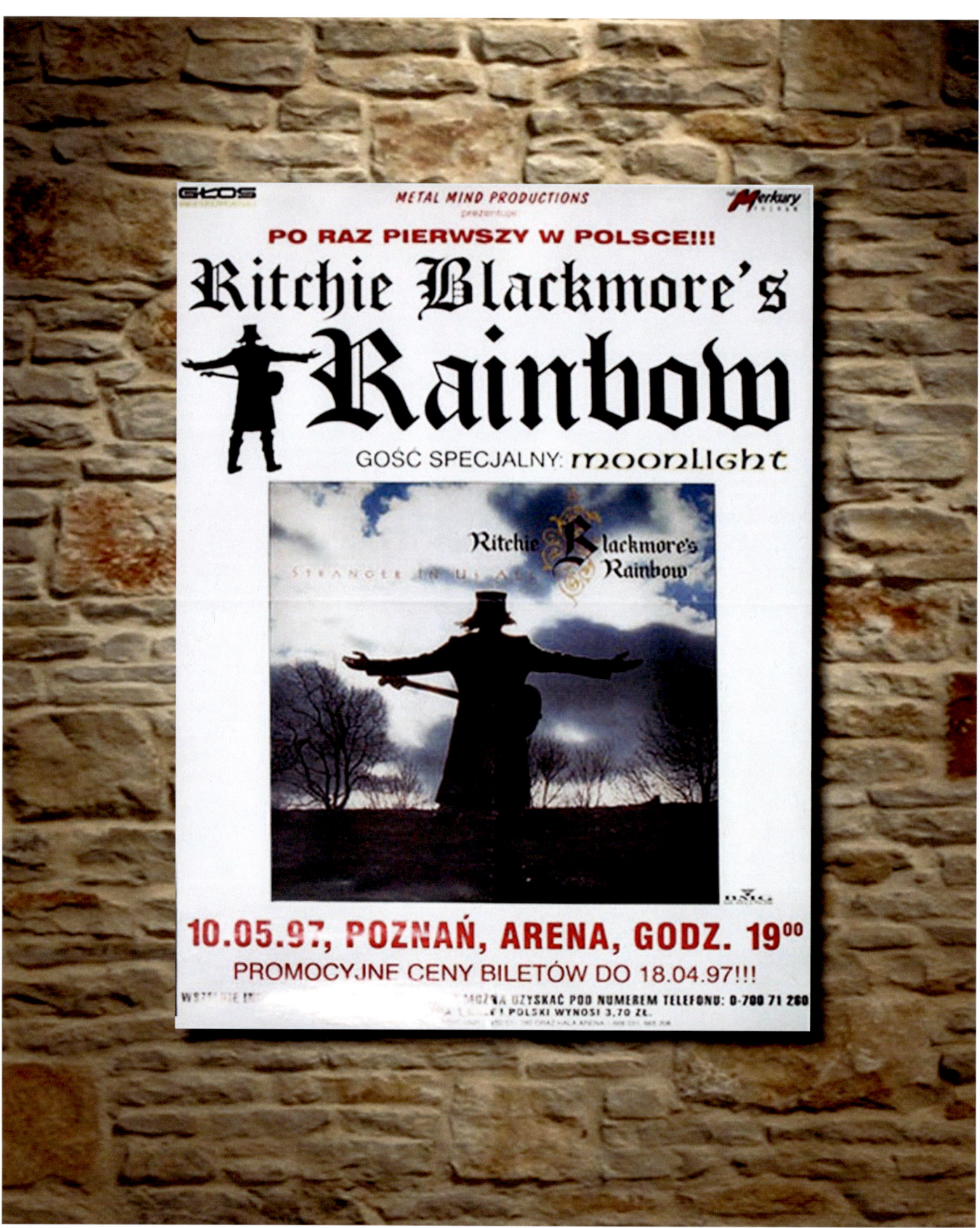

In The Shadow Of Times Past: 1997-

Since 1997 Ritchie has pursued a path that he had hinted at as far back as 1975. Eventually showing that he had the courage of his convictions by indulging in his passion for ancient music, blending Renaissance with even older medieval and early music influences but presenting it to an audience in a modern contemporary way. Blackmore's Night was born, a collaboration with Candice who used the stage name Night, the songwriting partnership was also free of the frictions that appear to have dogged his prior career, both with Purple and Rainbow.

Despite some of the inaccurate coverage from journalists, it wasn't solely acoustic. Indeed from the word go with the debut album *Shadow Of The Moon*, the Stratocaster was still very much in evidence and the same applied at the concerts where the odd Rainbow or Deep Purple track would be included at most shows.

At Schloss Eggersberg, 7th June 1997 as part of the promotional tour for *Shadow Of The Moon*.

The tour was due to start in Spain in September, however Ritchie had been suffering with a finger problem. A recurring situation that had something to do with the break he suffered way back in '87 whilst on stage with Deep Purple. His Doctor stated, quite categorically that he should not play the guitar for at least three weeks.

A memo was sent to all the promoters along with a copy of the Doctor's report. As such the European dates were put back, some falling by the wayside in the process and Blackmore's Night was launched on stage at the Nakano Sun Plaza Hall in Tokyo on 2nd November 1997.

After eight shows in Japan, gigs in Spain and Germany were played in December.

© Wymer (UK) Ltd

One of the more notable features of Ritchie's change in musical direction was also his willingness to be interviewed. Perhaps mindful of a need to explain what Blackmore's Night was about. One of the most extensive interviews took place in his then favourite restaurant, close to his home in Long Island called the Normandie Inn.

The interview for the UK *Record Collector* magazine took place in May 1998. It covered his whole career and lasted for close on four hours after which Ritchie gave an impromptu performance of some of the new songs.

© Neil Davies

At Schloss Eggersberg, Germany on 28th September 1998. Blackmore's Night hosted a private concert for a very limited number of fans. Even though information about it had been low key the proprietor was concerned that the castle could be besieged by hordes of fans so security guards were employed for the evening. Not only did that seem a little over the top but they were armed as well!

Sound check time at Waldeck, 14th July,

For the third tour of Germany, Ritchie managed to live out his fantasy to the full as the appropriately named Castle Tour was just that as they performed at castles across the country.

© Tobias Treichler

Throughout Ritchie's career there have been numerous controversies and dramas. The show at the Serenadenhof on 26th July 2001 saw one of the most bizarre events to occur. The venue, where Rainbow had played in 1996, is a courtyard within the never-completed Congress Building. Although it is an outdoor venue, it is not in a residential area and the 10 O'clock curfew seemed excessive. Ritchie clearly felt so and didn't want the show to finish so early. Consequently he locked the support band, Mostly Autumn in the backstage area, forcing them to start later than planned. When it came to Blackmore's Night, they played for nearly two hours, and pushed over the curfew by ten minutes.

Ritchie's tour assistant Richard Michaels went on stage ten minutes after the finish to explain that the band would love to play more but were not allowed. Half the crowd left but the other half continued to cheer for more and a full twenty minutes after leaving the stage, the band finally returned. They performed 'Writing on The Wall' and then 'Gone With The Wind' but a minute into the song the power was cut.

Unperturbed Ritchie switched to his twelve-string acoustic and he and Candice sat at the front of the stage and performed 'Now And Then' totally unplugged and virtualy inaudible except for a few people at the very front.

© Tobias Treichler

From Stratocaster to Hurdy-Gurdy. Stadthalle, Heidelberg, 23rd July 2002.

© Tobias Treichler

© Tobias Treichler

In 2002 as part of the German tour, two shows were played at Schloss Wartburg in Eisenach, the birthplace of Johann Sebastian Bach. Ritchie visited Bach's house and took a pebble from the garden as a "talisman" as he told the author at the time.

Schloss Wertheim, 7th August 2002

Friedreichsfen 2003

© Tobias Treichler

© Tobias Treichler

Burggaten, Rothenburg, 11th July 2003

© Wymer (UK) Ltd

Lucerna Theatre, Prague, 30th April 2006

© Heiko Langner

© Heiko Langner

125

Ritchie in Germany, 2007

As the years have rolled on, 2005 saw a new play on the life and work of Joe Meek that featured Ritchie's character, as played by Matthew Baynton. It was transposed to film in 2007.

The following year saw Ritchie get married to Candice on the 5th October in Long Island.

During an appearance on the German TV show Fernsehgarten on 17th July 2011, it was another chance to cross paths with old friend Andy Scott and his incarnation of Sweet. Their friendship stretches back over decades and Ritchie also performed on stage with Sweet back in 1976 as a tribute to Free guitarist Paul Kossoff.

© Jim Manngard

Back on the big stage under the Rainbow banner at the Stone Free Festival, O2 Arena, London. June 17th 2017

After two decades of seemingly finding his comfort zone with Blackmore's Night, Ritchie threw everyone off track when he announced in late 2015 that he would be putting a version of Rainbow back together for a handful of concerts. The decision to do the big rock shows again came after initially putting feelers out to Deep Purple but being rejected.

With a mixture of past and present Blackmore's Night members along with new vocalist Ronnie Romero, the first show at Loreley on 17th June 2016 was to an audience of around 25,000. It saw Ritchie's return to the arena size audiences as this 21st Century version of Rainbow presented a mix of Rainbow material that covered the seventies and eighties catalogue, with a similar mix of Deep Purple songs as well.

Taking things at a much more leisurely pace, just 15 shows were performed across Europe with the last being performed on 15th June 2019 as part of the Rock The Coast Festival at Fuengirola, Málaga, Spain. Live recordings were released but by 2021 Blackmore's Night released its eleventh studio album *Nature's Light*. Following the pandemic Ritchie has performed a few concerts as Blackmore's Night — all in the States.